Bahadir Kazakov

Bukharan Documents.
The Collection in the District Library, Bukhara

Translated from the Russian by
Jürgen Paul

Посвящается памяти

выдающейся исследовательницы мусульманских
исторических актов
проф. О.Д. Чехович
первооткрывательницы коллекции БОБ

и бывшего директора Бухарской Областной Библиотеки
М.М. Рахмановой
которая дала рукописям БОБ вторую жизнь в науке.

CONTENTS

Introduction		1
Bukharan Documents		7
1a	Documents from the earlier pre-colonial period	15
1b	Documents from the later pre-colonial period (1800-1868)	28
2	Colonial period (1868-1917)	30
3	The Bukharan amirate in political and economic isolation (1917-20)	42
4	Documents from the early Soviet period (1920-26)	47
Topography of chanceries		58
Appendix I		69
Appendix II		76
Bibliography		86
Reproductions		91

INTRODUCTION

The history of Central Asia from 1500 down to the Russian conquest in the second half of the 19th century remains poorly studied, even if new publications begin to alter the bleak picture drawn by Bregel[1]. Further efforts in putting new source materials at the disposal of researchers are needed, and documents should be of crucial importance in this matter. The administrative history of the Bukharan emirate as well as the khanates of Khiva and Kokand can only be written on the basis of documentary evidence, and the same holds true for social history (landholding patterns in the pre-colonial period being one of the central issues).

The collection of documents presented in this study is not the biggest one in Central Asia (or in Uzbekistan), it is surpassed, and by far, by the archives of the Bukharan Qushbegi now kept in the TsGIA in Tashkent.[2] Nevertheless, we are confident that

---

[1] Bregel, Yuri: *Notes on the Study of Central Asia.* Bloomington 1996 (Studies on Inner Asia : 26). New publications include the 3-volume series edited by Anke von Kügelgen and Michael Kemper: *Muslim Culture in Russia and Central Asia from the 18th to the Early 20th Centuries.* Ed. M. Kemper, A.v.Kügelgen, Dmitriy Yermakov. Berlin 1996 (Islamkundliche Untersuchungen : 200); *Vol. 2: Inter-Regional and Inter-Ethnic Relations.* Ed. A.v.Kügelgen, M. Kemper, Allen J. Frank. Berlin 1998 (Islamkundliche Untersuchungen : 216); *Muslim Culture in Russia and Central Asia Vol. 3: Arabic, Persian and Turkic Manuscripts (15th-19th Centuries).* Ed. A.v.Kügelgen, Aširbek Muminov, M. Kemper. Berlin 2000 (Islamkundliche Untersuchungen : 233); Florian Schwarz: *„Unser Weg schließt tausend Wege ein". Derwische und Gesellschaft im islamischen Mittelasien im 16. Jahrhundert.* Berlin 2000 (Islamkundliche Untersuchungen : 226) . Anke von Kügelgen's *Habilitationsschrift* also has to be mentioned in this context: *Inszenierung einer Dynastie. Geschichtsschreibung unter den frühen Mangiten Bucharas (1747-1826).* Bochum 1999. - Publications of hitherto unknown source materials include the *Kratkii katalog sufiiskikh proizvedenii iz sobranii Instituta Vostokovedeniia Akademii Nauk Respubliki Uzbekistan im. al-Biruni* (Berlin 2000). But the lacunae still are glaring and made even more evident by the publications quoted.

[2] See the present study, introductory remarks. The archives of the Khivan khanate are also extant see the preliminary study by P.P. Ivanov: *Arkhiv khivinskikh*

even a cursory glance at the present study will show that the collection kept at the Bukharan District Library is by no means to be neglected, neither by its scope nor by its contents.

The study itself is a description of the collection, not a historical investigation of the documents themselves. In our case, it is evident that the history of the collection itself would merit detailed investigation, since it is in a way significant that at the moment when it was converted from an „active" archive, serving the needs and interests of the government who compiled it, to a „scientific" one, serving the needs of historians (this moment occurred soon after the end of the Bukharan amirate), a commission made up of prominent Russian scholars of Oriental studies made its appearance who were asked to evaluate what had been found - there were lots of people around who could have told everything about it, but apparently they were not consulted. History had to start afresh..., and thus, the archive was transferred to the new center of power at Tashkent. Both parts, the majority of the documents now kept in Tashkent and those that stayed on in Bukhara, were however not really used, and they seemed „forgotten" for several decades. The Bukharan collection was discovered once again in 1940 only to get lost again, surfacing once more as late as 1984, and it is because of this complicated history that the author proposed that the study be dedicated to the memory of the two historians to whom these two discoveries are due. Thus, the history of the collection itself be used as one element in the history of Soviet historical science and its attitude towards the immediate pre-colonial past of Central Asia.

The issue most visible throughout the present paper of course is Bukharan administrative and social history. When trying to identify, e.g., names of offices, and determining their function, it soon became clear that the administrative history of the Bukharan amirate still remains to be written. This gap is most painfully felt for the 19th century. The extant basic studies date back to the 1920s, and no printed sources were available to us

---

khanov XIX v.: Issledovanie i opisanie dokumentov s istoricheskim vvedeniem. Leningrad 1940. The Kokand archives also have been described in a preliminary fashion: A.L. Troitskaia: *Katalog arkhiva kokandskikh khanov XIX veka.* Moskva 1968.

apart from the „administrative manual“ *Majmaʿ al-arqām* (it really is more like a short guide for administrative accountants and is more detailed on arithmetics than it is on administrative structures). The main body, the manual, was written around 1800 by a high-level official, Mīrzā Badīʿ. There is a sequel to this manual which contains a number of very brief descriptions of offices and their functions. This sequel has been ascribed to the same author and thus, to the same period. If this were true, it would be too early for much of the material described in the present paper. Bregel has very recently published a study on this source.[3] Bregel shows that the sequel to this „administrative manual“ cannot with the same degree of certitude be ascribed to the author of the manual, and that the question of when it was written has to be left open. This leaves the administrative history of the Bukharan emirate even more glaring a gap than it had been before. We had to rely on just this source for quite a number of details, above all explanations for offices and their functions. It is to be hoped that the Bukharan documents published here can be useful for future studies in this field, since it is clear that much of the history of the Bukharan emirate has to be reconstructed from documents.

Another problem we had to face is that many of the transactions reflected in the documents can hardly be linked now to social realities; the present study rightly concentrates on the archival form (diplomatic form of private legal documents) on the one hand and the legal contents on the other. In order to make the documents function as a tool for studies on social history, one would have to work not from so small a basis, but from the huge masses of documents known to be extant in their entirety. This type of study is still in its infancy as far as Central Asia is concerned, or, to be more precise, it still to has to be created. It is hoped that the present paper will offer some kind of incentive in this way.

The study first gives a general presentation of the collection. In the main part of the paper then, the documents are described in some detail. The material is broken down by periods: early pre-colonial until 1800, later pre-colonial 1800-68, colonial 1868-

[3] Bregel, Yuri: *The Administration of Bukhara under the Manghits and some Tashkent Manuscripts.* Bloomington 2000 (Papers on Inner Asia : 34).

1917, the Bukharan amirate in isolation 1917-20, early Soviet 1920-26 which thus includes the Bukharan People's Soviet Republic (1920-4), the Bukharan People's Soviet Socialist Republic (1924-5) and the first years of the Uzbek SSR. The chapters and paragraphs in this part of the paper have received continuous numbers. The following part reviews the documents by chanceries, arranged geographically. This part is a result of the archival need to classify documents according to issuing chanceries. In this part too, the individual chapters have been numbered throughout.

The paper has two appendixes. Appendix I is a glossary of terms used in the documents; in it, the state of the art with all its shortcomings is by necessity reflected. More precise translations and more detailed explanations cannot be given in this stage for the reasons stated above. Still, it is hoped that the glossary can serve not only for a better understanding of the present paper, but also as a starting point in further research in Bukharan administrative and social history.

Appendix II is a publication in facsimile and English translation of five documents from the described collection.

In transcribing quotations from Arabic, Persian and Turkī, the IJMES system has largely been followed. Turkī words are mostly transcribed without giving the correct phonetic value of the vowels. The language basically used in the documents has been called Persian in the translation following accepted international usage. Turkī has two main stages for the purposes of this paper: Chagatai and Uzbek; Uzbek was used as a term for most of the material after 1917 (with the measure of incorrectness this implies). Russian was transcribed in a simplified „anglophone" way in order not to encumber the translation with more than one system of translitteration. The system used in the Bloomington „Papers on Inner Asia" has served as a model here. All readers familiar with Russian will have no difficulty in identifying the Russian words intended.

A translation of a scholarly work produced in what is now a provincial town in Uzbekistan cannot be merely a translation. I have tried to supply extra references to literature published in Western languages or to editions of sources published outside the Soviet Union, but also to methodological implications. In both, I have tried not to be too intrusive, and my remarks have thus been reduced to the minimum; in this, I have aimed at making the text more useful for Western readers. The translations of the documents published here were made from the original Chagatay (document 1) or Persian (documents 2-5), with the Russian translation proposed by Kazakov as a starting-point; thus, all mistakes in these translations are my own. All of my additions to the basic text have been marked in the footnotes; some stylistic adaptations have however been made implicitly. The bibliography includes titles quoted by Kazakov and those added in the course of translating the paper.

Thanks are due to Dr. Florian Schwarz who read a preliminary version of the translation and made several valuable suggestions, and to Dr. Ildikó Bellér-Hann who helped with the English.

Jürgen Paul

BUKHARAN DOCUMENTS

The Bukharan museum has disposed of a collection of historical documents since the day it was founded. This collection is an old one and belongs specifically to the museum. It holds documents found at different times in the Bukharan *ark* (the citadel where the amirs of Bukhara were residing until their final demise in 1920). Most of the documents were discovered (by chance) in 1921, that is, soon after the end of the amirate. This collection included various types of documents of very different age. It had about 70 000 items. The government of the young Bukharan Republic[1] instantly took adequate measures in order to evaluate the findings (documents as well as books) and to ensure their safe-keeping. It invited a commission of specialists from Tashkent to Bukhara which counted among its members some of the best connoisseurs of Central Asian literature, as for instance A.E. Shmidt who was a prominent scholar in the department of Oriental studies in St Petersburg where he also had been trained. Shmidt had been sent to Tashkent in the beginning of 1920 and was asked to take the chair of the Turkestan Oriental Institute immediately after his arrival.[2] The commission was led by V.V. Bartol'd[3] who was staying in Tashkent at that time. The majority of the documents (and books) was transported to Tashkent and later formed the „Fond kushbegi amira bukharskogo" (The Qūshbegi[4] collection) in what is now the Central State Archive of Uzbekistan ЦГИА) where the documents are kept, together with papers

---

[1] The Popular Democratic Republic of Bukhara which existed from 1920 to 1924 when it was dissolved by the Bolsheviki (translator's note).

[2] On Shmidt's teaching and research in Tashkent, see *Istoriografiia obshchestvennykh nauk v Uzbekistane*, compiled by B.V. Lunin, Tashkent 1974, pp. 377-83.

[3] See ibid., pp. 100-6, on Bartol'd's activities in Turkestan. See also in B.V. Lunin, *V. V. Bartol'd.* Toshkent 1970, pp. 15-8, 28-30, 34-5, 59-60 (in Uzbek).

[4] For this and other technical terms, see the glossary at the end of this paper

pertaining to the Bukharan governmental archives which were integrated into the collection later on, under the shelf number F-I 126.[5]

A part of the documents found in the *ark* in 1921, however, stayed in Bukhara and were handed over to the museum which had been founded that very year. During the following years, several more old documents incidentally turned up in various parts of the *ark*; detailed information about the moments of these findings is available in the museum's inventory booklets. These documents together constitute the collection of the Bukharan museum.

Incidental discoveries of documents have occurred also in recent years. Thus, in 1977, when the author of these lines was the head custos of the museum, about thirty business letters were found in one of the *ark*'s cellars. These letters had been written by some Tatar students at Bukharan madrasas to their relatives in Troitsk in the southern Ural. Some time earlier, in 1953, comparable letters were found in the *gūrkhāna* (crypt) of the Mīr-i ʿArab madrasa.

Another part of the documents kept at the Bukharan museum stems from private persons, among them acquisitions made during the past few years.

The holdings of the Bukharan museum are all registered in the accession lists of the museum, numbered and classified according to a preliminary system. Additonally, a card catalog has been prepared, and some of the documents - above all the older ones, around hundred items dating from the 16th through 18th centuries - have been provided with their individual „passports" . In 1977, the museum started a scholarly inventory called „Manuscript documents".[6]

In the past, the scholarly processing and even the registration was awkwardly done, so that in some cases, legal ownership of the BOB[7] was not properly established. Errors were committed

---

[5] ФИ-126. - See G.Yu. Astanova, „Arkhiv kushbegi - vazhnyi istochnik". - In: *Obshchcstvcnnyc Nauki v Uzbekistane* (ONU), 1985 No. 7, p. 56.

[6] Документы рукописные in Russian, translator's note.

[7] BOB stands for „Bukharskaia oblastnaia biblioteka", the District Library of Bukhara (translator's note).

in identifying some documents; identical types of documents were not recognized as such and were thus differently called; the catalog cards were not filled out consistently; and last but not least, in a number of cases a single description (on a single card) covered several, sometimes even dozens of documents. That means that the registration documents for the old collection have to be revised in their entirety. But nevertheless, the registration as it stands today gives a fair impression of the collection, and it allows to affirm that the collection includes some pieces of major scholarly interest for the history of Central Asia. The collection in all runs into more than 2000 items.[8]

All the above-mentioned shortcomings have been taken into account in the description of the BOB's new collection which was relocated to the museum (from the BOB) in 1986.

The collection of documents from the BOB

Strictly speaking, the BOB's collection is not new. It was O.D. Chekhovich who discovered it in 1940 when she was in Bukhara as a member of the historical and ethnographic mission organized by the University of Tashkent (then still called Central Asian University) and led by M.S. Andreev.[9] Some years later, in 1954, she wrote: „This collection which in 1940 had not been described in any way, was later on described in Uzbek; this concerned about 400 items. But it seems that only part of the holdings were actually described".[10] In the end, an inspection of the existing documents proved this assumption (which was voiced by the scholar who first discovered them) to be true: the collection now holds about 600 items (sheets and scrolls). The above-mentioned mission had photographs made of some documents immediately. But perhaps due to the war, perhaps to the relocation of the library to a new building in

[8] A short description of the collection is B. Kazakov, „Kollektsiia istoricheskikh dokumentov Bukharskogo Gosudarstvennogo muzeia". - In: *Iz istorii kul'turnogo naslediia Bukhary.* Tashkent 1990, 62-78.

[9] M.S. Andreev, O.D. Chekhovich: *Ark (kreml') Bukhary.* Dushanbe 1972, 4-7.

[10] O.D. Chekhovich (ed.): *Dokumenty k istorii agrarnykh otnoshenii v Bukharskom khanstve.* Tashkent 1954, introduction, p. XXIII.

1971, the BOB collection got lost and was inaccessible to the specialists for forty years.[11]

In 1976, O.D. Chekhovich suggested that serious efforts be undertaken to find out about the collection's whereabouts, and this is what we did. But only in 1984 and due to the support of M.M. Rakhmanova who was then the library's director, the long lost documents were rediscovered somewhere in the magazines.

We began working with the documents when they were still kept in the library, starting with a preliminary identification of the papers and their equally preliminary systematization by type, place and year of composition, and we began describing them. Around 200 inventory cards were dressed, mostly for the oldest parts of the collection (pre-colonial period).

In 1986, the BOB collection was handed over to the Bukharan museum, and there, from 1987 to 1994, we completed the descriptions, above all those of the legal documents. In this long period, eight card catalogs were established in all: general (according to inventory numbers), according to years of composition, to chanceries, to addressees, to seals, and finally, according to subjects. The complete version of the description is given in the card files of the general catalog. It contains elementary information on every individual item: its type, emission information: date and place of composition and addressee; summarized contents of the document and intent of the transaction, the confirmation, the prescription or announcement; the attestations a document may carry: seals or signatures; paleographic information: type, fabric, size and color of the paper; type of handwriting and its size (approximately); quantity of lines, space between lines, presence and if applicable type of ornament, signs of envelopes for scrolls; the state of conservation of the manuscript in general.

Thus, the card file catalogs 2-8 have been established on the basis of the general catalog and consequently form specialized indexes.

[11] The most likely explanation for this is that the collection, in the process of its being moved, was by mistake transferred to another department, not to the department of manuscripts.

In 1986, we began establishing individual „passports" for every document in the BOB collection. These scholarly „passports" must be strictly individual, so that for every single document, a separate „passport" is established. Thus, if a sheet or scroll contains more than one document, every one of them still will receive its own „passport".

These „passports" are made up according to a unified pattern. Descriptions of documents of the same type consist of identical items, and moreover, these items are identical with the rubrics in the card file catalog. But of course, in the process of preparing these „passports" additional information and sometimes corrections have also been introduced.

There are more documents in the collections than there are registration units. This is because on some sheets and scrolls, additional acts linked to the original deed were written on the margin or on the verso. These are sometimes dated from the same period as the original text, but in the case of endowment deeds (*waqfīya*), they were mostly added later on. Thus, one scroll (registration number 327/491) is a long strip of locally made coarse cloth, on both sides of which four documents have been glued; they are all about endowing property as *waqf* to the benefit of the Bukharan mosque Mīr Ṭabīb. The first endowment deed was made out at the end of the 18th century, the last one in the beginning of the 20th.[12] There are several dozens of similar „mini-archives" (small series of documents) in the collection.

Taken together, all the documents in the collection run into around 700 - if we accept a wide definition of the term „document", thus including legal responsa (*fatāwā*), private correspondence, reports, petitions, financial and bookkeeping accounts, unconfirmed copies of official documents and so on. This means that our collection is quantitatively not a very big one, and as far as the sheer number of items is concerned, it

---

[12] B. Kazakov: „Dokumenty mecheti Mir-Tabib". - In: *Bartol'dovskie chteniia* 1990, tezisy dokladov. Moskva 1990, 35-37. See also B. Kazakov: „Analyse structurelle des actes de *waqf* provenant d'Asie Centrale, XIIIe - début XXe siècle (dans la perspective de l'établissement de modèles pour banques de données)". - In: *Cahiers d'Asie Centrale* 7 (1999), 211-232, with facsimile reproductions of the Mīr-Ṭabīb-documents. (Translator's note added.)

cannot be compared to such collections as the Bukharan *qūshbīgī* archives which include more than 100 000 documents according to a recent estimate.[13] Therefore it is impossible, on the basis of this collection, to draw general conclusions about all fields of administrative history: history of offices, of documentation, adjudication and so on - or other fields of social history which are habitually well represented in the archives. However, the material included in the collection allows us to ask a few questions concerning Central Asian documentary sources, diplomatics, sphragistics, paleography and above all legal documents (court records and notarial acts). This is mainly due to two favorable characteristics that prevail in the BOB collection: its large chronological scope and the very broadly differentiated types of documents it holds.

In the following, we will give some examples illustrating the general characteristics of the collection. First, the vast majority of the documents share the following features: they are written in Persian (the very few exceptions to this rule will be noted in due course), in the Arabic script (there is a very small number of Russian documents written of course in the Cyrillic alphabet) and only on paper which was either locally manifactured or imported (industrially produced), mostly from Russia. The ink used in the main - business - body of the texts is of the local black variety. Further features linking groups of documents will be mentioned in due course.

Chronology

As a result of the systematization and description of the documents in the BOB collection, it was established that the earliest document it holds is an endowment deed commemorating sheikh Saif al-dīn Bākharzī (d. 1261)[14] and drawn up

[13] Astanova, „Archiv kushbegi", 58.

[14] This date is taken from *Kitāb-i mullā-zāda*, lithographed edition, Novaia Buchara 1904, 41. - See Mu'īn al-Fuqarā, *Kitāb-i mullā-zāda*, ed. Gulchīn-i Ma'ānī, Teheran1339, 42. On this person, see J. Richard, „La conversion de Berke et les débuts de l'islamisation de la Horde d'Or." - In: *Revue d'Etudes Islamiques* 35 (1967), 173-184. - (Translator's note added).

by his grandson sheikh Yaḥyā.[15] It is known that the original of the deed was written in 736/1326, and the Bukharan copy was made in the second half of the 18th century (see below).

The most recent documents were written immediately before the Soviet takeover, and in particular a decree issued by the Bukharan amir ʿĀlim dated 1336/1918, and a purchase deed dated 1338/1920. The collection also includes a few documents pertaining to the Bukharan People's Republic (1920-24) and to the first years of the Uzbek SSR (1925-26).

Thus, the BOB collection spans 600 years of Central Asian history. It is however true that until now, not a single document dating from the 15th century has been discovered.

The collection can be broken down into five unequal parts by periods: 1a- earlier precolonial period until 1800, 1b- later precolonial period, 1800-1868, 2- colonial period, beginning with the day the Treaty of Bukhara, signed June 23rd, 1868, 3- the short period when the Bukharan amirate was politically and economically isolated following the founding of the Turkestan ASSR as a part of the Russian Soviet Socialist Federation RSFSR (beginning with November 1st/14, 1917), 4- documents from the beginning of the Soviet period in the history of Uzbekistan, when the *qāḍīs* were still in office and all private business was conducted and documented according to traditional (i.e., hanafite) law.

Of course, there were substantial differences in the social and economic situation prevailing in the Bukharan amirate, the Bukharan People's Republic and the Bukhara/Zeravshan district.[16] For the study of documents it is important to note that the general changes were duly reflected in the documents' form,

---

[15] B. Kazakov, „Opyt opisaniia aktov". - In: *Materialy soveshchaniia po vostochnoi arkheografii.* Moskva 1990, 84-7. - On the history of the Kubravī current in Central Asia, including the shrine of Sayf ad-Dīn and his *khānaqāh* at Fatḥābād, see Devin DeWeese, „The eclipse of the Kubravīyah in Central Asia". - In: *Iranian Studies* 21 1-2 (1988), 45-83. - Yaḥyā is best known for his work, *Awrād ul-aḥbāb wa fuṣūṣ al-ādāb*, part 2, ed. Īraj Afshār, Tehran 1345, which he wrote for the inmates of this *khānaqāh*. - (Translator's note added).

[16] The *oblast'* (district) of Bukhara was formed on January 15, 1938; down to that date, from the inauguration of the Uzbek SSR in 1925, the region constituted the Zeravshan district.

above all the private ones. Some of these changes will be illustrated below.

1a Documents from the earlier pre-colonial period, until 1800

There is a relatively restricted number of documents dating from the earlier pre-colonial period down to 1800, numbering no more than about fifty items, including a group of documents compiled on a large scroll written at the end of the 18th century. This scroll was not transferred to the museum and is at present exhibited in the Department of Oriental Literature of the BOB as a specimen for the culture of writing.

The document going back deepest in time is, as has already been stated, a copy of the endowment deed to the benefit of the mausoleum and the *khānaqāh* of Saif ad-dīn Bākharzī. The Bukharan copy was written in the second half of the 18th century, as O.D. Chekhovich established in her study and complete edition of the document.[17] However, she committed a minor inaccuracy here. A seal was imprinted to the scroll at the places were the individual sheets were glued together (88 pairs of imprints in all), and Chekhovich read its inscription as „Amīr Maʿṣūm b. amīr Dāniyāl Bī“ and drew the following conclusion: „The handwriting, the paper used and the seal all point to the last quarter of the 18th century.“[18]

In fact, the name on the seal imprints (in the central circle) is to be read slightly differently, as „Maʿṣūm ibn amīr Dāniyāl“ (to be discerned comparatively clearly at lines 56-7 and 63-4), that is, the name Maʿṣūm occurs without the title *amīr*. In other terms, the copy was made when the heir apparent had not yet ascended the throne.[19] Moreover, the seal imprints are dated

[17] O.D. Chekhovich, *Bukharskie dokumenty XIV v.* Tashkent 1965.

[18] Ibid., 25-6.

[19] The Manghit rulers Dāniyāl Bī Ataliq and his son Shāh Murād (called Amīr i Maʿṣūm, the „sinless ruler“) reigned from 1172/1758 to 1199/1785 and from then to 1215/1800, respectively. - C.E. Bosworth, *The* New *Islamic Dynasties*, Edinburgh 1996, 292. For an appreciation of early Manghit history and historiography, see Anke v. Kügelgen, *Inszenierung einer Dynastie:*

1188/1774-5 (this date appears particularly clearly at lines 67-8).[20] On the whole, thus, Chekhovich's dating was correct.

When O.D. Chekhovich first saw the Bukharan copy in 1940, the scroll apparently was undamaged. At least, she did not mention any defects in her short description.[21]

Today, the scroll is damaged, it has fallen apart into two fragments of unequal length, and a portion of the text between the two fragments has been lost. O.D. Chekhovich gives the length of the scroll as 48,70 meters.[22] The two fragments together are 47,75 meters long, and depending on whether Chekhovich included the leather cover or not (0,47 m), the lost part measures from 0,48 to 0,95 m. When comparing the text on the extant fragments with the edition, the lost portion in our scroll makes up 24 lines.

The first fragment of the extant manuscript is glued to a cover in the form of a lengthened triangle, made of brown leather. This cover was adorned with paper rosettes and cartouches which were colored green and had an ornament stamped on it. On some of the stamp imprints, a name can still be read: Mullā Ḥakīm b. mullā Muḥammad Raḥīm (maybe the bookbinder). Along the borders of the lengthened triangle, longish scraps of yellow (golden) paper had been glued to the leather, equally decorated. Most of these have separated away from their support.

As a special feature of the Bukharan copy of the endowment deed drawn up in favor of the mausoleum and *khānaqāh* of Saif al-Dīn Bākharzī, it has to be noted that there are no attestations at the bottom of the text. No judge imprinted his seal, nor did any witnesses seal or sign it. In the same line, there is no invocation formula at the beginning. It was obviously for this reason that O.D. Chekhovich stated that this

---

Geschichtsschreibung unter den frühen Mangiten Bucharas (1747- 1826). Bochum 1999 („Habilitationsschrift"), forthcoming in the *Beiruter Texte und Studien* series, Steiner Verlag, Stuttgart. - (Translator's note.)

[20] A date on a seal impression of course furnishes a *post quem* date. Some rulers in fact had „immobilized" dates on their seals, whereas judges and other officials changed their seals rather frequently. - (Translator's note with comments due to Florian Schwarz.)

[21] O.D. Chekhovich, *Bukharskie dokumenty*, 33.

[22] Ibid., 25; but it is not stated whether the length of the leather cover is included.

was a copy without beginning and end.[23] Here it is maybe useful to cite an analogous case. In the earliest of the *waqf* endowments mentioned before, those in favor of the Mīr Ṭabīb mosque (inventory number 327a/491a), the same defective form can be observed. This deed was drawn up in 1793-4, when Ma'ṣūm b. Dāniyāl already ruled in Bukhara (1785-1800).[24] The document is a duplicate of an earlier deed, maybe the primordial one, which was written down at an unknown moment. Both texts start with the „business" part, leaving out the protocol. In the second deed, the seals (judge and witnesses) are equally missing. And in this case as well, the points where two sheets were glued together were confirmed and protected by the seal of Ma'ṣūm b. Dāniyāl (unfortunately, not a single one of the imprints can be read).[25] This coincidence raises the question whether it was an accepted rule in the last quarter of the 18th century to include into copies and duplicates of documents, at least of endowment deeds, the „business" part only.

As was stated before, there are no documents from the 15th century in the BOB collection. There are two pieces dating from the 16th century. The earlier one (inv. number 16/6) is a decree (*yārlīq*) issued by the Shībanid ruler Naurūz Aḥmad (r. 1552-6).[26] It was written in the Chaghatay language in 963/1556 and addressed to one of the *sulṭāns* (the members of the ruling Chingizid house) named Muḥammad Hāshim.[27] This text is noteworthy for a number of reasons. First, in its external appearance it does not convey the imprint of a ruler's decree. It is written on a rather small sheet of paper (29x18 cm) of inferior quality, and the handwriting is not royal, either. Apart from a short formula of invocation and the

---

[23] Ibid., 26.

[24] *Istoriia narodov Uzbekistana* vol. 2, 1993, 214.

[25] Kazakov, „Opyt opisaniia aktov", 86-7.

[26] Bosworth, *Dynasties*, 288 gives 1552-6; this is confimed by A. Burton, *The Bukharans* (Surrey 1997), 557. It is established that Naurūz Aḥmad died in Ḏū 'l-qa'da 963/September-October 1556, and the year is also given in his funeral inscription. See B. Babadjanov, A. Muminov, J. Paul, *Schaibanidische Grabinschriften*. Wiesbaden 1997, German part p. 109. On the Shībanids in general and their particular system of rulership, see the corresponding article in the *Encyclopedia of Islam* (R. McChesney). - (Translator's note.)

[27] For comments on this document, see Appendix II, document no. 1.

intitulation formulae, the text is written in an unappealing *nastaʿlīq* hand. Another particular feature is the additional remark in the right margin, made in the name of the sender in a very informal style reminding one of family letters and written also in a very casual hand. The subject matter is equally unusual. In it, a certain *qāḍī* Saiyid Muḥammad Shafīʿ is elevated to „the most high position to the right hand side". This means that this person is given a high rank in the retinue of the addressee.

In spite of the fact that this decree issued by Naurūz Aḥmad shows many features of informal communication, it still conforms to the accepted standard form for official documents. All its elements are present: the invocation, the intitulation, the formula of public promulgation, the addressee, the disposition and so forth, and at the end, as parts of the eschatocol, the date and the seal imprint.[28] Let it be noted that the ruler's seal is imprinted as is the rule in official documents at the top of the page, below the name of the khan, in the middle of the sheet, to the right of the short lines 3 and 4.

In the text of this decree, there is a formula rarely found in Central Asian official documents announcing that this decree will be confirmed (corroborated) by the ruler's seal, it is called a *muhrlūq nishān* („sealed decree").

The text itself offers two terms for its genre as a document, the Turkic *yārlīq* (line 5) and the Persian *nishān* (lines 9 and

[28] The standard form of official Turkic documents was studied by L. Fekete (*Bevezetés a hódoltság török diplomatikájába*, Budapest, 1926) A. Zajączkowski and A. Reychman (*An outline history of Ottoman diplomatic/Zarys dyplomatyki osmańsko-tureckiej*, Warszawa, 1955) and others. Arabic decrees from the Fatimid period were studied by S.M. Stern (*Fatimid decrees. Original documents from the Fatimid chancery*. London, 1964). Short studies of Arabic, Persian and Ottoman official documents are given in the background article „Diplomatics" in the *Encyclopedia of Islam*, (Björkman, Reychman, Zajączkowski and others). Serious studies in this field were presented by the Soviet orientalists A. Grigor'ev (on Chingizid diplomatics: *Mongol'skaia diplomatika XIII-XIV vv (Chingizidskie zhalovannye gramoty*. Leningrad 1978) and M.A. Usmanov (on Juchid documents: *Zhalovannye akty Dzhuchieva ulusa*. Kazan' 1979). - This is not the place to add full references for Oriental or Turkic diplomatics. As far as Central Asia is concerned, a look into Bregel's bibliography is useful (*Bibliography of Islamic Central Asia*. Bloomington 1995, vol. 2, p. 1041 sqq.). (Translator's notes added.)

15), both meaning „order", „decree", „disposition". And indeed, the given text is - formally as well as in its contents - an order displaying the features of a semi-official letter. The document is reproduced here in facsimile with English translation in Appendix II, number 1.

At the end of the 17th and in the beginning of the 18th centuries two purchase deeds concerning state land were concluded. The deeds also document the process by which part of the transferred lands were exempted from taxes. In both documents, the promulgator is the Bukharan ruler Subḥān-qūlī Khān (ruled 1680-1702, from the Ashtarkhanid or Toqay-Temurid or Jānid dynasty).[29]

The earlier (inv. number 570/477, dated 1697) is particularly remarkable. Before we give its typological features, a look at its legal contents is in order.

The essence of the transaction documented in it is as follows: a fixed portion of some state land to be sold to a private person is simultaneously exempted from all taxes. This final action which is the real goal of the whole procedure is preceded by two other transactions: In the first transaction, Subḥān-Qulī Khān sold two pieces of state land (*zamīn-i mamlaka*), situated in Kish province (presently the Kashka-dar'inskaia *oblast'* in Uzbekistan). As usual, all plots bordering on the sold land are identified in detail (lines 12-14, 15-17). It is important to note the area of each sold plot, the first one is given as 5 *juft-i gāw*(line 11) and the second as 10 *juft-i gāw* (line 15, for the purposes of this paper, it is not essential to have the area in modern measures).[30] Thus, the two plots were sized 1 : 2.

---

[29] *Istoriia narodov Uzbekistana* vol. 2, 1993, 213. (See also Bosworth, *Dynastics*, 290-1, and Burton, *Bukharans*, genealogical tables 552-5, and her chapter on Subḥān Quli's reign, 329-362. - Translator's note added).

[30] On the term *juft-i gāv* see P.P. Ivanov, *Khoziaistvo dzhuibarskikh sheikhov*. Moskva 1954, 10 (note 4); E.A. Davidovich, *Materialy po metrologii Srednei Azii*, Moskva 1970, 122. (The term literally means „one yoke of oxen" and is used for an area which can be cultivated in an agricultural annual cycle with such means. It is therefore not possible to translate it into square meters or acres. See also B. Fragner, „Social and internal economic affairs", in *Cambridge History of Iran* vol. 6, Cambridge 1986, p. 492, and J. Paul, „Le

The second procedure was the following: now that the two plots of land sold had become taxable private property *milk* (subject to the *kharāj* type of land tax),[31] the ruler (*ān 'ālī ḥaḍrat*) took over (*giriftand*) the second plot which was twice as important in size and yield as the first one with the consent of the buyer (*mushtarī*) in lieu of *kharāj* payments due from the first plot, thus exempting the smaller plot in perpetuity from all regular land taxes (lines 21-3). In other words, the second plot was formally alienated again out of the formal ownership of its buyer back into the state holdings as a compensation for all future *kharāj* payments due from the first plot.

The third procedure: „For the specified reason (*sabab*), the above-mentioned first plot (*maḥdūd*) has become the buyer's (*mushtarī*) free private property (*milk*), exempted from land tax (*khāliṣ az kharāj*)" (lines 23-4).

It was O.D. Chekhovich who discovered and studied this document type and the transaction thus concluded.[32] Two features should be described more in full, even if they are not unique to this document.

The person who formally acted as purchaser of the state lands was Khudāyār Bī b. Khudāyqūlī Bī. He was a powerful figure in his time, just as his father also had been.[33] The price for the transaction, that is, for the two plots of land, was one copy of

---

village en Asie Centrale aux XVe et XVIe siècles". - In: *Cahiers du monde russe et soviétique* 32 (1991), 9-17. For the whole question of landholding in Central Asia, including taxes, rents, their relative importance and meaning, including the type of deal presented here, the following article is of prime importance: E.A. Davidovich, „Feodal'nyi zemel'nyi milk v Srednei Azii XV - XVIII vv.: sushchnost' i transformatsii". - In: *Formy feodal'noi zemel'noi sobstvennosti i vladeniia na Blizhnem i Srednem Vostoke.* Bartol'dovskie chteniia 1975 g. Moskva 1979, 39-62. - Translator's note.)

[31] The *kharāj* was the normal type of land tax in Central Asia and amounted to the double of the *'ushr* or *dahyak* or tithe. Davidovich comes to the conclusion that *kharāj* property owed a regular 20 % of the income as tax, another 10 % of the harvest going to the owner as rent, see previous note. (Translator's note.)

[32] O.D. Chekhovich, *Dokumenty k istorii agrarnykh otnoshenii v bukharskom khanstve. Vyp. I: akty feodal'noi sobstvennosti na zemliu XVII-XVIII vv.* Tashkent 1954 (all published), in particular XV-XX (in the editor's introduction).

[33] Ibid., 84-86 for the text and Russian translation of a document (*vaṯīqa*) issued for Khudāyār.

the Qur'ān (lines 18-9). This was not exceptional either, quite a few similar cases have been published by O.D. Chekhovich.[34] In the corroborating parts of the document, it is striking that there is a number of witnesses which would be unusual for a private transaction - 44 imprints of seals. (For the sake of comparison, we adduce here the number of imprints of seals in the documents studied by O.D. Chekhovich: doc. 10, 17 imprints; doc. 11, 4 imprints of one seal; doc. 12, 45 imprints; doc. 18, 29 imprints; doc. 19, 4 imprints.) It is tempting to link the high quantity of imprints to the high social position of the purchaser.

Among the owners of the seals we have first of all the khan himself, and alongside the high *qāḍī*, two more lower level *qāḍīs*, some members of the ruling dynasty (on the imprints, only *sulṭān* can be read as a part of these persons' titles), 11 representatives of high-ranking Turkic families (as evident from the title *bī* mentioned at the end of their names), some more notable figures (as identified by the mention *khwāja* going with their names or such components of names as *al-Ḥusainī*), and some holders of high offices at court (*dīwānbīgī*, *muftī* and so forth).[35]

The document was written in Persian on cream-colored oriental paper, the sheet is sized 50x32 cm, the main body of the text has 29 lines. It is written in a fairly tall and bold *nasta'līq* hand with some elements of *dīwānī*. Black ink was used. The names of the khan and his father are extrapolated to the right margin and written in gold. The document is

[34] Ibid., documents 19, 21, 25, 40. (See also the study by Davidovich, „Feodal'nyi zemel'nyi milk"; translator's addition).

[35] Some of the imprints of the seals can be given here. Seals beneath the text, in the left margin. Oval seal of the *qāḍī*-notary, 35 : 39 mm, *aqḍā al-quḍāt qāḍī mīr Nāṣir b. qāḍī [Mīr-i] Mīrān b. qāḍī Mīr ['Abdallāh] al-Ḥusainī (1094)*. The same seal is found on another document, see Chekhovich, *Dokumenty agrarnyx otnoshenii*, list of seals no. 38. Ruler's seal (acting as selling part in the transaction), black and white drawing glued in the upper right margin, almond-shaped seal, 26 : 21 mm, *Saiyid Muḥammad Subḥān-Qūlī bahādur Khān 1096*. Seals of witnesses in the lower right margin, 42 imprints in all, for example: oval seal, 21 : 27 mm, *Ghāyib Naẓar ataliq b. [...] 1103*; square seal, 19 mm, *Muḥammad Hāshim b. Muḥammad 'Ābid Khwāja*; square seal, 34 mm, *amīr Shams ad-dīn b. Aḥmad qāḍī amīr Saif ad-dīn al-Ḥusainī 1099*, oval seal (unclear), 19 : 29 mm, *Niyāz Muḥammad b. [...]begī bī 110X*; oval seal, 17 : 23 mm, *Allāh-berdī b. Qūchqār bī*.

damaged: In many places, the paper is torn, particularly at the right margin, the end was torn off and is consequently lost.

In the BOB collection, there are three documents hailing from the first quarter of the 18th century, two of them are purchase deeds.

The earlier one (inv. number 17/3) was written down in 1116/1704. The document takes act of the declaration made by the seller in the presence of the rightful deputy judge (*ba-ḥuḍūr-i nā'ib-i shar'ī-yi qāḍī*) in the city of Samarqand and the surrounding countryside (lines 9-10). The seller declares that he is acting at the same time as legal owner of his own property and as attorney for some female relative (whose name is given, but the degree of kinship is not indicated, lines 10-12).

The transaction concerns three plots of land (tax category *dahyak*, „tithe"). These plots were apparently situated next to one another, since the features mentioned to define their borders (rivers or canals *nahr*, other plots of land, a public street *kūcha*, a mosque and a minor canal *jūy*) are enumerated not separately for every single plot, but for all three at the same time.

The price is given in a rather complicated currency, *tanga-yi dah dū nīm-i rā'ija*, „silver coins of two and a half in/to ten current at the present moment" (line 19)[36].

Beneath the text in the right margin, there are 27 imprints of seals, the majority of which are illegible. Among them, the seal of the officiating *qāḍī* can be found, together with some other judges who acted as witnesses. Some more witnesses came from notable families (as evident from the title *mīr* preceding their names) or were religious officials (as for instance the *muftī* whose title can be read on one seal) or else, members of leading Sufi (as for instance the *Aḥrārī*)[37] or from

---

[36] See the remarks given below with the translation of the document, Appendix II, number 2. (Translator's note.)

[37] For this family - who descended from the noted Samarqandi sheikh of the 15th century, Khwāja Aḥrār - see McChesney, „The amirs of Muslim Central Asia in the XVIIth century." - In: *JESHO* 26 (1983), 33-70. - The *Aḥrārī* family was

noted Turkic families (as indicated by the title *bī*). The corroborative part of the document contains, together with the seals, a list enumerating 12 more witnesses whose names can only partly be deciphered.

The document was written in Persian and has 29 lines in all. The handwriting is *nastaʿlīq* with some elements of *dīwānī*, written in a large, space-consuming style with drawn-out letters. Black ink was used, and the paper is thick, cream-colored, of oriental artisanal making. The document is in a satisfactory state of conservation. It is published as no. 2 in Appendix II.

The second purchase deed was drawn up in the same place in 1126/1714 (inv. number 178/495) for the purchaser Allāhyār b. Allāhbirdī Bī. This man was - as his father had been - one of the richest figures in the Ashtarkhanid khanate, and the present deed was not the only one by which we know of his extensive acquisition of agricultural and other lands. O.D. Chekhovich has published thirteen documents showing the expanse of his landed properties.[38]

The document under discussion takes act of Allāhyār's acquiring a whole village in the *tūmān* of Shāwdār (Samarqand province, to the SE of Samarqand city, line 9) which before belonged to six persons. These persons apparently came from a military and/or bureaucratic background. This is indicated by the forms of their names which are followed by official titles, such as *chuhra-bāshī* or *chuhra-āqāsī*, and also by the general attribute going with them: *shujāʿat-āthār va mubārizat-aṭwār*, „courage-marked and warlike".

The price of the purchased land is given in a *tanga*-currency of equally complicated designation as was the case in the previous one: *tanga-yi dah sah-nīmī*, „silver coins of three and a half in/to ten".

As in the first purchase deed, there are a lot of seals in the corroborative section of this document. Beneath the text and to the right and below the great circular seal of the sitting

far from being the most influential Sufi family in this period, as McChesney rightly states. (Translator's note.)

[38] O.D. Chekhovich, *Dokumenty*, author's introduction.

judge there are 19 oval seals of witnesses (the biggest one is 20x30mm, the smallest one 15x23 mm). The seals are imprinted in the right margin, on the level of lines 11-18, number 6 imprints in all, and there are oval as well as square (19mm) and circular ones (31mm).

The document was written in Persian, it consists of 21 lines, the handwriting is *nastaʿlīq* with elements of *dīwānī*.

On the right margin, running perpendicular to lines 15-21, there is a two-line *fatwā* confirming the deed.

The document was written on a particularly large sheet (71,5 x 24,5cm) which was produced by gluing two sheets together. The first (upper) sheet is made of thicker paper and is furthermore glued on to a solid piece of paper; the second (lower) sheet is narrowing down to 22,5cm. To the upper part of the document, a cover in the form of a lengthened triangle was glued, the cover is made from brown soft leather and measures 28x27 cm, it becomes narrower towards the point where it was glued to the paper (25cm).

Another document (inv. number 296/226) from the same period, the first quarter of the 18th century, is dated 1130/1717-8, but it represents another type. It is a confirmation of a land grant issued in favor of a certain Saiyid Naṣrallāh Khwāja „in accordance with the ordinances (*aḥkām*) and decrees (*asnād*) issued by the great khaqans" (lines 3-6).

The document under discussion is remarkable for the office the promulgator held. As is shown by the seal, the document was issued by a judge (the name cannot be read on the imprint). We know numerous decrees and grants, official documents issued on behalf of the rulers, khans or amirs by provincial governors or semi-independent regional princelings who were only formal vassals of the rulers in Bukhara,[39] or

[39] A.A. Egani, O.D. Chekhovich, „Regesty sredneaziatskikh aktov." - In: *Pis'mennye pamiatniki Vostoka* (PPV). Yearbook, 1974, 1975, 1976-7, 1978-9, published Moskva, 1981-7. The items are arranged in current numbers throughout the series, references are thus made to numbers of documents; doc. 36, 37, 43, 45, 47.

their sons,[40] and also by officials residing in the capital, the chief *ṣadrs* or others.[41] But no case of a *qāḍī* acting in this function seems hitherto to have been known.

The second remarkable feature of this document (a feature lacking in similar confirming decrees of later periods), is the very peculiar form in which the right of the favored person to receive a renewed version of a previous grant is stated (the *constatatio*): *ba-mawjid-i tajdīd chak-i sharʿī tafwīḍ namūdīm*, „We issued this legal document in order to renew [the grant previously issued] and handed it over [to him]" (line 5).

The third particular feature of this document is that it gives more legal weight to the previously issued documents than to the actual one. We read: *az maḍmūn-i aḥkām wa asnād-i qadīm dar naguzārand*, „let them not transgress what was decreed in the old ordinances and documents" (line 9).

Yet another special feature of this document is the formula by which the author legitimizes himself; this formula likewise does not occur in later documents. He says: *bahr-i ḥukm wa-farmān-i humāyūn*, „in accordance with the order and decree of the ruler". For the sake of comparison, we'll adduce some other formulae serving a similar purpose, they present other elements and are of course different due to their being written in Turkī: *ḥaḍrat-i khān ḥukmīdīn*, „by the khan's order",[42] or *ḥaḍrat-i khān ḥukmīdīn Niẓām al-Dīn ... dādkhwāh sūzīm*, „by the khan's order, Niẓām al-Dīn *dādkhwāh*, my word"[43], or

[40] Ibid., doc. 91, 92.

[41] Ibid., doc. 5, 8, 19, 29.

[42] Ibid., doc. 68.

[43] Ibid., doc. 71. (*Dādkhwāh* was a title for an official who was in charge of transmitting petitions and complaints to the ruler and also of announcing the ruler's decisions to the petitioners. He also could hold some military command. See Mīrzā Badīʿ Dīwān, *Majmaʿ al-arqām*, fol. 92b. - In a publication which came to my notice during the preparation of this translation, Bregel has shown that the sequel to the *Majmaʿ al-arqām* cannot now be dated with the same measure of certitude to the years around 1800 as Vil'danova and others had done (Bregel, *The Administration of Bukhara*). Bregel also discusses the way this source is employing certain administrative terms; in the context of this paper, the discussion of *qūshbigi* has prime importance (see note 73). Nevertheless, in the notes to this translation as well as in the glossary, administrative terms have more often than not been explained according to the very brief definitions given in the sequel to *Majmaʿ al-arqām*. This shows how badly in-depth studies of Bukharan administration in the

ḥaḍrat-i shāh ḥukmīdīn ... sūzīm, „by the shah's order, my word".[44]

There is a last remarkable feature in the document under discussion. The text has a self-identification, it is called *chak* (line 5) which in this context must mean „legal document".[45]

Another document which is unusual in many respects is dated from the end of the 18th century (inv. number 18/7, dated 1197/1783). It is a purchase deed, written probably in the Bukharan *tūmān* of Pāy-i rūd (as is evident from the places mentioned in the body of the document).

The peculiarities begin with the fact that the chancery where this document was drawn up is not mentioned. In some other purchase deeds from Samarqand (dating likewise from the end of the 18th century), the chancery is typically identified.[46] On the other hand, among the published documents from this period there are some examples of provincial deeds which do not mention the chancery. These originate from Kish province[47] and also from the *tūmān* of Shāwdār in Samarqand province.[48]

It is perhaps interesting to note that the purchase deed of 1783 brought together people from a similar social position. Both parties were craftsmen (*ustād*), the plot of land was sold by *ustād* Shāhnaẓar and purchased by *ustād* Qalandar (line 2), and before the owners of all the plots next to the sold object (they had to be mentioned in order to exactly define what was sold), we also read the designation *ustād* (line 4 sqq.).

In the corroborating section of the document, we have a surprisingly large number of witnesses, there are 12 names,

---

decades immediately preceding the Russian conquest are needed. - Translator's note.)

[44] Ibid., doc. 56.

[45] Normally, *chak* is used for a purchase deed which is also proof of ownership, especially of real estate, or else a document used in the transfer of money (translator's note). But the term is also known to mean a „written and signed sentence of a judge or magistrate" (Steingass, *Persian-English lexikon*).

[46] O.D. Chekhovich, *Dokumenty*, doc. 23, 26, 28, 30, 34.

[47] Ibid., doc. 24, 38.

[48] Ibid., doc. 17, 33.

whereas the object of the transaction is of relatively modest dimensions: a garden of one *ṭanāb* and a half (line 3).[49]

Another interesting feature about this document is that on the verso there is a note confirming that the purchaser mentioned in the main document renounced to a case he had brought to court against his son. The object of the case and the sum paid in compensation are specified: the case had been revolving around a pond (*ḥauḍ*) which probably was situated in the garden, and some trees planted around it (*lab-i ḥauḍ*). 3 gold coins *ashrafī* were paid in compensation for withdrawing the lawsuit. This note is kept in a very much shortened form, it is devoid of legal and procedural formulae, it is not dated and does not carry any corroborative instruments.[50]

Another document from the end of the 18th century is the copy of an endowment deed in favor of the Bukharan mosque of Mīr Ṭabīb (inv. number 327a/491a, dated 1794-5), see above page 11.

[49] A *ṭanāb* or *jarīb* is a area of not altogether clear dimensions, probably between four to six *ṭanāb* in a hectare. - Even if documents made out for the ruler, for court officials and notables as a general rule show the seals or signatures of many witnesses, this can also be the case with the rank-and-file people. - (Translator's note.)

[50] However, the legal formula by which the withdrawal of the suit is declared is given in full: *dar badal-i īn mablagh [...] da'wa gudhāshta ibrā'-i dhimma-yi ān namūdam*, „in return for payment of this sum, I declare the suit withdrawn and the claims made therein fulfilled".

1b Documents from the later pre-colonial period (1800 - 1868)

There are about 60 documents dated to the end of the pre-colonial period (1800-1868). They are significantly more varied in form and contents as the earlier pieces. In this group, almost all types of documents we know from earlier periods are to be found. There are purchase deeds (inv. number 577/479, dated 1222/1808; inv. number 576/478, dated 1265/1848), endowment deeds in their basic form (inv. number 162/145, dated 1231/1816) and some variants, as for instance a renewal of an endowment (inv. number 177/159, dated 1235/1820), and other types of documents concerning *waqf* properties (inv. number 312/241, dated 1283/1866-7 and others). Private documents abound, there is a marriage contract, accompanied by testimony of witnesses as to the conclusion of the marriage on the verso (253/190, dated 1228/1813), a *qāḍī* document concerning the exchange of a bridal gift (*mahr*) for a specified sum (278/215, dated 1242/1827).

Moreover, among the official documents preserved from the last decades of the pre-colonial period, we find almost every known type: two decrees issued by the Bukharan amir Naṣrallāh (295/225 and 25/64, both dated 1242/1827; it is perhaps interesting to note that they were confirmed by two different seals, their form is identical, but the inscriptions are different), a *qāḍī* document issued on the amir's order concerning the distribution of *'ushr* lands (50/5, dated 1248/1831) and other ordinances issued by the amirs (470/385, dated 1251/1835; 312/241, dated 1283/1866).

One of the innovations introduced into chancery practice during the first half of the 19th century was the use of European (factory made) paper. Thus, the above-mentioned decision of a *qāḍī*, dated 1831, was written on a sheet of factory made greenish paper with water marks; a piece of paper on which a divorce was confirmed by witnesses (385/307, dated 1274/1858) was manufactured in Russia and carries a factory stamp (the text on the stamp is illegible, however).[51]

[51] Kazakov, „Opyt opisaniia aktov", 84-7.

2 Colonial period (1868 - 1917)

Nearly half the documents in the BOB collection belong to the colonial period, around 300 items in all. This is quite natural, since the nearer we get to our time, the more documents can be supposed to have survived. Broken down by decades, we get the following distribution:

1870s - 19 items

1880s - 32 items

1890s - 39 items

More than 50 documents probably dating from the closing decades or years of the 19th century or the first years of the 20th do not carry exact datings and must therefore be left out from this list.

1900s - 127 items

1910s - more than 150 items; again, around thirty of these are not dated by the year, but can be attributed to the beginning of the 20th century (by internal evidence).

The colonial part of the BOB collection presents the full range of types known for Central Asian official and private documents. There are around 30 types of legal documents alone (variants and subtypes not taken into account); other documents make up 17 further types.

Here, we will give a simple account of the types of documents extant from the colonial period, separately for legal and other documents.

2.1 Legal documents

2.1.1 Private documents, notarial acts

2.1.1.1 Contracts of lease (real estate): 38/53, dated 1322/1904; 268/205, dated 1330/1912

2.1.1.2 Withdrawal of action taken in court for compensation: 61a/37a, dated 1315/1898; 69/9, dated 1324/1906

2.1.1.3 Withdrawal of action taken in court without compensation: 140v/123v, dated 1316/1899, 128b/111b, dated 1333/1908

2.1.1.4 Act documenting the extinguishing of a debt: 353/276, dated 1333/1915

2.1.1.5 Act recognizing the rights of a third party: 67/31, dated 1314/1896

2.1.1.6 Acts renouncing claims: 454a/369a, dated 1309/1891; 104/87, dated 1318/1900

2.1.1.7 Act parcelling out property held in common: 452/367, dated 1315/1897

2.1.1.8 Waiver of a part of a heritage: 424/341, dated 1333/1915

2.1.1.9 Act about a revision taken of a minor's property held in guardianship: 400/317, dated 1322/1905

2.1.1.10 Letter of authorization (to act as attorney for a third party): 84/15, dated 1319/1901; 71/26, dated 1334/1915

2.1.1.11 Marriage contract: 76/23, dated 1326/1908

2.1.1.12 Endowment deed (*waqf-nāma*): 52/488, dated 1308/1891; 154/137, dated 1331/1913

2.1.1.13 Donations: 48/43, dated 1304/1887; 346/269, dated 1330/1912

2.1.1.14 Certificate of indebtedness: 86/13, dagted 1328/1910; 80/19, dated 1333/1914

2.1.1.15 Pawn tickets: 479/394, dated 1295/1878, 224/163, dated 1334/1915

2.1.1.16 Purchase deeds: 471/396, dated 1286/1870; 237/174, dated 1334/1916

2.1.1.17 Receipts: a) about having received compensation for action taken in court: 61b/37b, dated 1315/1898; b) about having received property after the death of a person who had died without heirs[52]: 35/56, dated 1313/1896; c) about having received repayment of a loan: 73/26, dated 1325/1907; d) having received a loan: 342/265, dated 1326/1909

2.1.1.18 Testimony about the conclusion of a marriage: 252b/190b, dated 1228/1813

2.1.1.19 Testimony about a divorce: 578/480, dated 1285/1868

2.1.1.20 Certification of the obligation of a woman not to give her daughter in marriage without her elder sister's consent: 82/17, dated 1329/1911

2.1.2 Court decisions concerning property[53]

2.1.2.1 Decision fixing the annual allowance for an orphan[54] as well as naming a guardian for him, 342a/265a, dated 1324/1907

2.1.2.2 New fixing of this allowance, addition to the previously mentioned decision: 342b/265b, dated 1326/1909

2.1.2.3 Naming a female guardian (*waṣīya*) as well as a legal representative (*amīn*): 375/297, dated 1336/1917

2.1.2.4 Handing out sequestered property (taken to court after the death of a person who had died without heirs): 480/395, dated 1325/1907

2.1.2.5 Division of inheritance (numerous cases, for instance): 560/474, dated 1303/1885, 387/309, dated 1334/1916

2.1.2.6 Decision taken in court in a legal case concerning property: 583/309, dated 1334/1916

2.1.3 Official documents with legal consequences

2.1.3.1 Grant (жалованная): 350/273, dated 1336/1917

[52] Such property was handed over to the *qāḍī* who kept it as long as possible heirs might still present themselves. (Translator's note.)

[53] The question of how notarial acts documented at the *qāḍī*'s office are to be distinguished from court decisions is addressed in the second part of this paper on the systematization of the documents. See the preliminary publication, B. Kazakov: „Vidy sredneaziatskikh aktov". - In: *Pamiatniki istorii i kul'tury Bukhary.* Vyp. 4, Bukhara 1995, 71-6.

[54] Orphans could not freely dispose of their inheritance as long as they were minors. The guardian had to represent them in all legal matters. But the *qāḍī* was to see to it that the guardian did not squander the wealth of his ward, and that on the other hand, the minor received what was suitable to his social position. (Translator's note.)

2.1.3.2 Decrees of the Bukharan amirs (numerous documents, e.g.): 260/197, dated 1305/1887, 403/321, dated 1328/1910

2.1.3.3 Ordinances of the Bukharan amirs (numerous documents, e.g.) 406/324, dated 1285/1868-9; 305/235, dated 1308/1890

2.1.3.4 Ordinances of court officials: 469/384, dated 1302/1884-5; 559/473, dated 1312/1894-5

2.1.3.5 Passport for a trip from Bukhara to Russia, 516/431, dated 1332/1914.

Thus, among the documents from the colonial period, nearly all types of legal documents known to Muslim jurists can be found. For instance, Bulgakov asserts that in a formulary going back to the 12th-century jurist an-Nasafī, 30 types of legal documents are described.[55] In the BOB collection, there are 26 different types since some types mentioned by Bulgakov are missing. These are: annulation of a transaction (Bulgakov's type 2), a document affirming advance payment for merchandise (Bulgakov's type 3), a document on sums given at the receiver's free disposal (Bulgakov's type 5), four subtypes of documents manumitting slaves (Bulgakov's types 19-22). Besides, Nasafī has two subtypes of attorneyship (23-24), two subtypes of certificates of indebtedness (25-26), and two subtypes of donation (27-28). Thus, in Nasafī's formulary we have of course the concept of „type" as was current in the author's day. On the other hand, we are grouping legal documents according to the legal transaction included therein. For instance, all variants and subtypes of sale make up only one type, and the differences in the social status of the vendor (*bā'i'*), whether acting as the owner of the sold commodity or as attorney or guardian and so forth, are not taken into account, nor is the material form of the sold commodity: arable land, a house or whatever. All these can serve for delimitating subtypes or smaller groups within the broader types of documents. These questions will be addressed in the section of the paper dealing with the systematization of the BOB collection.

[55] P.G. Bulgakov: „Formuliary dokumentov po chastnomu pravu". - In: *Materialy po istorii Srednei Azii.* Tashkent 1991, 69.

The official documents represent the full range of traditional types, but in addition, due to the new social and political circumstances, they have also a new type of document, the „international passport".[56]

As far as paleography is concerned, the documents from the colonial period present the following features: imported factory-made paper is used on a large scale, mainly Russian paper. A clear simplification of the rules governing the drawing up of legal documents can be observed. For instance, instead of a complete invocation formula, merely a symbolic sign is used.[57] In many of the decisions, and also in the ordinances issued by the amirs, the seal is imprinted on the verso. In quite a few numbers of private documents, the corroborative part ends with the formula *ḥuḍḍār al-majlis* „people present at the session" without giving the names of the witnesses.

2.2 Private documents (private papers)

Among the papers from the colonial period preserved in the BOB collection, quite a few types of private documents and papers are to be found. It is perhaps useful to give a brief description of some of the most frequently represented types, since in the present paper, no section is devoted specifically to the analysis of their structure and their interpretation.

2.2.1 Official letters[58]

2.2.1.1 Letter written on behalf of the Bukharan amir Muẓaffar (as indicated by the seal) to his son Mīr ʿAbd al-Muʾmin who was then governor of a frontier province. The amir is assigning his son two tasks: first, to ascertain the fate of the

[56] This type may pre-date the colonial conquest. „Passports" are transmitted in formularies (*inshāʾ*-collections) as early as the pre-Mongol period, see Heribert Horst, *Die Staatsverwaltung der Großselǧūqen und Ḫorazmšāhs*. Wiesbaden 1964; and in another (Timurid) collection edited by Roemer, there are other examples of documents called „passports", see Hans-Robert Roemer, *Staatsschreiben der Timuridenzeit: Das Šaraf-nāmä des ʿAbdallāh Marwarīd in kritischer Auswertung*. Wiesbaden 1952. (Translator's note.)

[57] This sign is an abbreviation for the formula *huwa* and can be found in a very large number of later documents. (Translator's note.)

[58] The elements distinguishing offical letters from ordinances and decrees will be discussed in the second section of this paper.

sons of Khudāybirdī *mīrākhūr*,[59] second, to send the proceedings of the customs station on to the capital. The text of the letter is written in two columns. At the top of the sheet, a formula of invocation. Dated at the bottom left corner of the sheet. Sealed (by the amir) on the verso. Factory-made paper, 20x12cm. 306/236, dated 1300/1883.

2.2.1.2 Letter written on behalf of the Bukharan amir ʿAbd al-Aḥad (as indicated by the seal) to the *qāḍī* ʿImād al-Dīn, confirming that a petition written by the addressee had reached the court and that a person who was proposed by the *qāḍī* had been appointed *āqsaqāl*[60]. Invocation at the top of the sheet, dated beneath the text in the left corner, sealed by the amir on the verso, text in two columns, factory-made paper. 22x12cm, 401/319, dated 1315/1897.

2.2.1.3 Letter written on behalf of a court official (*maḥram*) to a certain highly placed person (*īshān-i ṣudūr*[61], name not given), inviting this person to a celebration (*tūy*) held at the palace (*dawlat-khāna*). Text written in two columns, invocation above the text, dated beneath, no seal, factory-made paper, 35x16cm, 0/370, 1336/1917.

2.2.2 Financial and economic papers with government or palace background

2.2.2.1 Report and account written on behalf of a government official (indicated by contents) to the amir (judging by the formula used in the address, name not given), announcing that construction activities have been carried out successfully on three sites. Quantitative indicators and types of work are enumerated as well as the names of masters (craftsmen) employed. No date, no seal. Factory-made paper, 32x15cm. 0/197, datable to the end of the 19th or the beginning of the 20th century.

---

[59] *Mīrākhūr* was the title of the chief equerry, in control of the ruler's stable. Mīrzā Badīʿ Dīwān, *Majmaʿ al-arqām*, fol. 95a. (Translator's note.)

[60] Literally, „white beard", village elder or rural notable; Persian *rīsh-safīd*. (Translator's note.)

[61] *Īshān* is a common form of addressing people of high(er) rank; the *ṣudūr* was an official supervising the pious foundations *awqāf* outside Bukhara; his colleague, the *ṣadr*, was in charge of the urban endowments including the immediate neighborhood of the city. See *Majmaʿ al-arqām* fol. 88a. (Translator's note.)

2.2.2.2 Financial account submitted by four officials (*mulāzimān*, names given), enumerating the proceeds of tax collection or other tax income. No seal, no date. Factory-made paper, 44x18cm. 0/492, end of 19th-beginning of 20th century.

2.2.2.3 List of military units under command of the writer (units of ten), with enumeration of soldiers' names and their commanders (commanders of ten, *dah-bāshī*), the lists of names are grouped under the names of commanders. No seal, no date. Factory-made paper, scroll, 258x18cm, 0/308, end of 19th-beginning of 20th century.

2.2.2.4 Report of an official residing in the capital (as indicated by contents) addressed to a high-ranking official, enumerating three kinds of duties in eight administrative units and institutions. On the verso, names of seven madrasa teachers (*mudarris*) who may be candidates for a vacant post. No seal, no date. Factory-made paper. 22x12cm. 0/228, end of 19th-beginning of 20th century.

2.2.2.5 Account of expenditures submitted by a finance official (indicated by contents, name not given) to a high-ranking official (going by the address formula), defining the allowances in kind handed out to some officials (*ʿāmil*) from the income of the government depositories or caravan-sarais. No seal, no date. Factory-made paper, 26x15cm. 0/436, end of 19th- beginning of 20th century.

2.2.2.6 Notes taken about various goods handed out from larder and/or granary, among others to the palace kitchen, with mention of weight, quantity or other measure, and also of price in Russian roubles (*sūm*). Diary. No seal, no year (entries dated by day and month only). Factory-made paper. Beginning and end are missing. 0/475, end of 19th-beginning of 20th century.

2.2.3 Petitions

The samples of this type of document in the BOB collection can be broken down into variants according to the social and political status of their addressees and authors.

2.2.3.1 *ʿĀriḍa*[62] written on behalf of a high-ranking person (going by the contents, neither name nor rank given in the text) and addressed to the ruler (indicated by the formulae used in the address), asking to be raised to the rank of *banāras-pūshān* „dressed in Benares cloth". No invocation, no seal, no date. Factory-made paper, 23x11cm, 0/411, end of 19th-beginning of 20th century.

2.2.3.2 *ʿArḍ-i bandagī* written on behalf of a provincial official (neither name nor rank given) and addressed to a prince or a high official (judging by the address), expressing his feelings of guilt and regret and hopes of forbearance; in the following, the writer describes his poor situation and asks for a pension (*rutba*) or a salaried position. On paleographic grounds, this is probably a draft. Factory-made paper, 27x18cm, no seals nor date. 0/147a, end of 19th - beginning of 20th century.

2.2.3.3 *ʿArḍa-dasht* written by an elderly scholar (judging by the contents, no name given) to a *muftī* (no name given), asking the *muftī* to see to it that the writer be given some lodging in Bukhara or in the vicinity so that he might pass „the rest of his days" with „his heart at ease", praying for the ruler's well-being. No invocation, no seal nor date. Factory-made paper, 29x16cm, 0/58a, end of 19th - beginning of 20th century.

Among the documents drawn up during the colonial period, there are about 20 demands and suits.[63] This type of document is not analyzed in the present paper in its particular structure, and therefore only some examples will be briefly described in what follows. They are not legal documents in a strict sense since they are not issued by a *qāḍī* but rather addressed to a court or a *muftī*.

2.2.3.4 Complaint written by one Ḥaidar-qūl to the supreme *qāḍī* (judging by the formula used for the address, name not given) against one Muḥammad-Naẓar, living at Jūy-i naw,

---

62 This term and the following ones (*ʿarḍ-i bandagī* and *ʿarḍa-dasht*) are all synonymous, and all imply a report going with a plea or petition. (Translator's note.)

63 These documents have a special form. For an example from the 19th century, see Kazakov, „Dokumental'nye pamiatniki Srednei Azii". Tashkent 1987, fig. 9 (a facsimile reproduction of such a document).

Nasaf province. Essence of the complaint: The defendant refuses to pay back some money the plaintiff had given him as a loan; the plaintiff demands that the defendant be forced to pay back the loan. - Beneath the text, as with all complaints, a short question to which the addressee is asked to respond by way of a *fatwā*, written in the same hand: „Is there in this question something which corresponds to the sharia or not?" - Beneath this note, a circular seal, 39mm, mullā Muḥammad Yūsuf b. mullā Muḥammad Ṣāliḥ al-muftī, dated 1291. Above the imprint a note written by the jurist: „Yes, and God knows best" (*bāshad huwa al-aʿlam*). Factory-made paper, 17x22cm. 139a/122a, no date. - The date can be established by the imprint of the seal above the *fatwā* which is dated 1291, and the disposition of the amir which in turn is dated 1293. The document must thus have been written between these two years, 1874-6. - On the verso of the paper, the disposition taken by amir Muẓaffar (identified by his seal) was written down, addressed to the judge of Nasaf province, *mīr* Badr ad-Dīn: „Investigate into this case and decide". Beneath this disposition, the withdrawal of the suit is taken act of.

2.2.3.5 Complaint filed by the moneylender Dawrā Yahūdī with the supreme *qāḍī* (judging by the formula used in the address) against the debtor Muḥammad Nabī. Beneath the text, the formula of the *fatwā*. Beneath that, imprint of a circular seal, 46mm, Mullā Mīr Muḥammad mudarris ṣudūr b. Ākhund Mullā ʿAbdalḥakīm ṣadr, 1321. - On the verso, disposition by the ruler, and beneath that, act of withdrawal, dated 1326. - Going by the two mentioned dates, the complaint was written between them, 1903-8. Factory-made paper, 17x22cm. 128/111.

2.2.4 Fatāwā

Fatāwā are to be found in all chronological layers of the BOB collection. This kind of document is well known,[64] and therefore it does not have to be explained in this paper.

However, there are about ten *fatāwā* in the BOB collection deserving special attention: they were written on demand and

[64] See *Islam. Entsiklopedicheskii slovar'*. Moskva 1991, 252.

according to the Shiite variety of Islamic law. These documents are also interesting in their outward appearance: On the paper, the demand for a *fatwā* takes up the center and constitutes the main body of text, whereas the decision is written near the top in small script and in short lines (553/467, not before 1302/1884 and 546/460, not before 1308/1890 and other examples).

2.2.4.1 Demand for a *fatwā* addressed to a jurisconsult (as seen by the title *Ḥujjat al-islām*, name not given): „Please explain in detail the methods to avoid usury (*ribā*): which is the easiest and smoothest path to prudence?" The text omits all data of expedition: no date, no place of composition, no name. No invocation nor seal. The last four lines (and therefore the seal also) are missing. 547a/461a, four lines. - The response (decision, *fatwā*) reads: „When in a transaction (*mu'āmala*) one part is in weight or size less than the other one, and this deficit makes up a significant amount (*māliyyat*), then the transaction becomes valid (*ṣaḥīḥ*) if the lesser part is augmented [...]". -Beneath the text, seal imprint of this *faqīh*, oval, 11x15mm, ʿAlī al-Jaʿfarī al-Ḥusainī, 1308. - Factory-made paper, script: the demand was written in accurate *nastaʿlīq*, the decision in cursive. 547/461, not before 1308/1890 (as shown by seal).

2.2.5 Private letters

Private letters are yet another type of private documents. In the BOB collection, there are about 80 items representing various types. More than 60 out of these can be dated to the colonial period.

In diplomatics, private letters are counted among the documentary sources when defined broadly.[65]

The majority of letters in our collection do not give any expedition data, that is, the name of the sender, the place and date of sending are missing as well as the address. Some examples seem to indicate that this information was written on

[65] See A.S. Lappo-Danilevskii, *Ocherk russkoi diplomatiki chastnykh aktov.* Petrograd 1920, p. 11. (For letters in oriental diplomatics, see art. „Correspondence" in *Encyclopedia Iranica* [Ahmad Tafazzoli and Hashem Rajabzadeh]. Regrettably, there is no article on Persian diplomatics in the *EIr* so far, neither under „Diplomatics" nor under „asnād". Translator's note added.)

the „envelopes": The paper on which a letter was written was made into a scroll which at its top was covered up by another scrap of paper. On this scrap, half the sender's seal was impressed, and to the left of the imprint, the title or honorific of the addressee was written. The name was never mentioned in accordance with the well-known rules of Central Asian etiquette. For instance, the inventory number 522/428 can be dated by the imprint of the half seal on the „envelope".

The absence of the addressee's name and address on the letter is easily explained by the simple reason that letters were habitually sent with a messenger or another person making the trip for some reason or other, so that it was not necessary to indicate the addressee in writing.

One letter was preserved in a European envelope with the sender's half seal on the verso side, impressed where the corners are glued together. To the left of the imprint, again, the titles of the addressee: 510/425, not before 1323/1905-6 (dated by the seal).

Private letters can be divided into several types according to the following features: the social status of the sender, the social status of the addressee, and the subject matter of the letter. As examples, we will present some types of letters.

2.2.5.1 Demands, petitions. In demands and petitions, the writer normally asks to be appointed to a salaried position or else to be supported in some affair or other. In this group, there are 9 items, for instance, 535/449 (end of 19th - beginning of 20th century)

2.2.5.2 Accompanying letters. These are letters sent together with either a present or some object the addressee had been asking for (or anything else). 7 items, e.g., 497/412, dated 1917.

2.2.5.3 Felicitations. Felicitations are sent on occasions such as the addressee's appointment to a certain position, a promotion in titles or some honor being conferred to him. 4 items, e.g., 0/20 (end of 19th-beginning of 20th century).

2.2.5.4 Orders. Orders given by non-official persons are 2 items, for instance, a letter ordering the addressee to give the bearer of the letter a horse with specified features, capable of pulling a carriage, 0/312a, 1915.

2.2.5.5 Letters expressing loyalty to patrons residing in the capital, 4 items, e.g., 0/6 (end of 19th - beginning of 20th century).

2.2.5.6 Letters expressing gratitude for various benefits, 8 items, e.g., 505/420 (end of 19th - beginning of 20th century). The letter preserved in a European envelope (mentioned above) also belongs into this group.

2.2.5.7 Letters giving information. This is the largest group of letters in the BOB collection, 29 items in all, and they differ in various respects from the rest of the group (see above). - In the following, one specimen of this group will be described in some detail: Letter written by one Mullā Saiyid Khwāja (name/title to be read on the seal impressed on the „envelope"), Charjuy, to a certain *mudarris faqīh* (as written on the „envelope"), Bukhara. Name of addressee not given. In it, the writer informs the addressee about the end of a dispute between some peasants on the one hand and Turkmens belonging to the Yomut tribe on the other hand, and also about the former *qāḍī* of Charjuy having moved to Qarshi; the writer was on bad terms with this *qāḍī*. - The paper on which this letter was written was rolled up to form a thin scroll and put into an envelope made of paper. On the envelope, the quoted information on sender and addressee. Factory-made paper, 22x16cm, text in two columns, script: bold *dīwānī*. 522/428, not before 1327/1909-10 (date of seal).

2.2.5.8 Among the private letters there are the following additional types: invitations (0/293a, end of 19th - beginning of 20th century), condolence (537/451, end of 19th - beginning of 20th century) and some more.

3 *The Bukharan amirate in political and economic isolation (1917-20)*

The documents dating from the period 1917-20 include about fifty items representing the same types of documents as have been described for the preceding periods. Here, only the types can be enumerated.

3.1 Private legal documents

3.1.1 Purchase deeds. About a dozen, e.g., 372/295, dated 1336/1918; 141/124, dated 1338/1920.

3.1.2 Pawn tickets. 3 items, 191/140, dated 1337/1917 and two more.

3.1.3 Lease documents, more than 20, e.g., 190/139, dated 1337/1919, 432/256, dated 1338/1920.

3.1.4 Certificates of indebtedness. 3 items, e.g., 58/40, dated 1338/1920; 37/54, dated 1338/1920.

3.1.5 Different types of *qāḍī* documents, 14 items. Among these:

3.1.5.1 Document testifying about derelicts (left by a person who had died without heirs) having been handed over, 456/371, dated 1336/1918;

3.1.5.2 Receipt about rent received, 439/355, dated 1337/1919;

3.1.5.3 Note about alleviating a debt by expenses not regulated in the original contract, 436b/352b, dated 1337/1919.

3.2 Court documents. 5 items, among them a legal decision dividing up an inheritance, 380/302, dated 1337/1918

3.3 *Waqf* (endowment) deeds.[66] 3 items.

3.3.1 Endower Qurban-Bay; act concerning one *ṭanāb* of land located in one of the Bukharan suburbs in favor of the Ḥusainiyya of Ḥājjī Shaikh 'Abd al-Khāliq. Beneath the text,

[66] On the formular of endowment deeds see O.D. Chekhovich, „O diplomatike", in: *Istochnikovedenie srednevekovogo Vostoka*. Moskva 1984, 228.

3.3.1 Endower Qurban-Bay; act concerning one *ṭanāb* of land located in one of the Bukharan suburbs in favor of the Ḥusainiyya of Ḥājjī Shaikh ʿAbd al-Khāliq. Beneath the text, seal of *qāḍī* ʿIẓām ad-Dīn, oval, 37x46mm, dated 1335/1916-7. Names of 5 witnesses. 23 lines of text. Oriental paper, cream-colored, 50x21cm. Black ink. Main body of text written in *nastaʿlīq*, Arabic quotations and formulae in *naskh*. 468/383, dated 1336/1918.

3.3.2 Endowment deed presenting the same features as the preceding one, that is, it carries the same date, the seal of the same *qāḍī* has been imprinted, and the endowment is made in favor of the same Ḥusainiyya and written on the same kind of oriental paper. However, the endowment is made by a different person, Aḥmad Āqsaqāl, and it is written in another hand, a large *dīwānī*, the paper is much larger, 28cm - the sheet is as long as the preceding one. 146/129, dated 1336/1918.[67]

3.4 Official documents.

3.4.1 Appointment deed by amir ʿĀlim, appointing ʿUmūr-qūl-bī to the office of *mīrākhūr*[68].The intitulation is complete and has at its end the *turkī* formula *sözimiz* „Our word/order". The amir's seal was imprinted on the verso, in lower right corner, circular, 33mm (the legend is illegible).[69] 11 lines of text with large spaces in between, written in a large and careful *nastaʿlīq*. Oriental paper, cream-colored, 60x27cm. 266/203, dated 1336/1918.

3.4.2 *Farmān* issued by amir ʿĀlim and addressed to the supreme *qāḍī* Burhān ad-Dīn, ordering him to find out whether a supplicant (name and title given) has the right and qualification to be appointed *mutawallī* (administrator) of some *waqf* lands in the place of the deceased incumbent. At the top edge of the list, a symbolic trait as invocation formula

---

[67] A Ḥusainiyya is a room or building designed for the Shiite ʿĀshūrāʾ mourning ceremonies during which the murder of Ḥusain (at Kerbela in 680) is lamented. The two last documents thus take us into the Shiite community of Bukhara, made up essentially of persons of Iranian origin. - (Translator's note.)

[68] Chief equerry. See Glossary, Appendix I.

[69] On the standard form of official documents see Chekhovich, „O diplomatike", 227-8.

huwa al-ḥaiy.[70] The amir's seal was imprinted on the verso, in the bottom right corner, circular, 22,5mm, „Saiyid amīr 'Ālim". Factory-made greyish paper. The document has suffered from moisture. 18x11cm. 11 lines of text and one line in the margin. Written in a beautiful small *nasta'līq* hand, black ink. 307/237, dated 1337/1919 at the end of the text.

3.4.3 *Farmān* issued by the *dīvānbīgī*[71] Ghulām-Qādir (as read on the seal) to the *qarāul-bīgī*[72] Dāniyāl, ordering him to immediately send 20 *mann* of barley as fodder for animals to Qurgan. Text written in two columns, the second part being the narrower column to the right. 8 and 5 lines of text. Above the text, the mentioned symbol serving as invocation. Written in negligent *nasta'līq*, getting larger to the end. Factory-made yellowish paper. 22x11cm, 10/77, dated 1338/1920. Fully dated at the end of the text.

3.4.4 Official accompanying letter, written by the chief scribe of Khiva to his homologue in Bukhara (going by the formulae used in the address, no names given), asking him to give a written answer, confirmed by a seal, to a question on law, explained in a separate letter which was sent with the carrier (the letter explaining the legal question is not extant in the BOB collection). Text written in *turkī* in two columns, 23 and 16 lines of text. Seal of sender at the bottom, oval, 24x29mm, „Mullā Bābājān makhdūm b. dāmlā Ṣafarniyāz Khwārazmī", 1337/1918-9. Factory-made paper, cream-colored, 27x16cm. *Nasta'līq*, black ink. 226/164, dated 1338/1919.

3.4.5 Passport allowing its carrier to leave the city of Bukhara, issued by the chief *qūshbīgī* (*kull-i qūshbīgī* as in the legend of the seal) for David Āqbāsh. The carrier is allowed to travel to Khāṭirchi with his merchandise. Issued at the *wizārat-i Bukhārā.* At the top edge, a registration number. Sealed by a half seal beneath the text, rectangular seal, 15x41mm,

---

[70] „He is the Living One". A specimen of such an abbreviated sign is published in Kazakov, *Dokumental'nye pamiatniki*, fig. 14 (facsimile of text).

[71] Head of civil administration, especially of the chanceries and the treasury as explained by Vil'danova in the glossary to her edition of *Majma' al-arqām*, p. 115. - (Translator's note.)

[72] He was in charge of maintaining security in the country, in particular he had to watch over the roads. *Majma' al-arqām*, fol. 94b. - (Translator's note.)

„Niẓām ad-Dīn khwāja bī kull-i qūshbīgī“.[73] The year is illegible. 8 lines of text, *nastaʿlīq*, black ink. Paper with the

[73] This title has not been sufficiently explored, and there is considerable confusion over it. Semenov says that the title *qushbegi-yi kull* was first bestowed on Tūraqūl Bī, son of a slave, in 1709 during the reign of ʿUbaidallāh Khān the Ashtarkhanid („Bukharskii traktat o chinakh i zvaniiakh“. - In: *Sovetskoe Vostokovedenie* 5 [1948], 137-153, p. 139.) In his translation of the *ʿUbaidallāh-nāma*, he does not give the Persian expression, but the Russian *verkhovnyi kushbegi* only (Mīr Muḥammad Amīn-i Bukhārī: *ʿUbaidallāh-nāma*. Russian translation by A.A. Semenov, *Ubaidulla-name*. Tashkent 1957, p. 210 and once more, p. 276, referring to another incumbent). The phrase *velikii kushbegi* is used in *Majmaʿ al-arqām* for the Persian *qūshbīgī-yi kalān*, fol. 92b and translation, p. 97. *Majmaʿ al-arqām* was written in the last years of the 17th century C.E. with additions in the very first years of the 18th, and thus is earlier than the report of the *ʿUbaidallāh-nāma*. For the dating of the sequel of *Majmaʿ al-arqām* (in which the brief definitions of offices and their functions are given) see Bregel's recent paper and the brief statement in note 43. - M.A. Abduraimov gives the fullest discussion of the title in *Ocherki agrarnykh otnoshenii v bukharskom khanstve v XVI - pervoi polovine XIX veka*. Tom 1, Tashkent 1966, p. 75-81. He sees two offices: one is the (Russian form) *kushbegi*, „head falconer“ as the title is usually explained, this fits with the explanation given in *Majmaʿ al-arqām*. Another is the (Russian form) *koshbegi*, derived not from the Turkic word for „bird (of prey)“, but from the word for *khanskaia stavka*, the ruler's (military) camp. Abduraimov uses the title *verkhovnyi koshbegi* quite a lot, but does not give conclusive evidence for the Persian *qūshbīgī-yi kull*. See also Bregel's article „Kosh-begi“ in the *Encyclopedia of Islam*. - The matter is further complicated by the fact that in the second half of the 19th century, people in Bukhara distinguished a *qūshbīgī-yi bālā* „upper *qūshbīgī*“ who was identical with the *qūshbīgī-yi kull* and resided in the Ark (the citadel) who acted as deputy for the ruler and thus was a kind of Prime Minister (Semenov's terminology) from a *qūshbīgī-yi pāyān* „lower *qūshbīgī*“ residing at the entrance to the Ark, and thus well below the former (see Abduraimov, *Ocherki*, 81-2, and Semenov, *Ocherk pozemel'no-podatnogo i nalogovogo ustroistva b. Bukharskogo khanstva*. Tashkent 1929, p. 44). - This discussion shows that at least some titles as well as the offices behind them and the whole administration of the Bukharan emirate clearly need further study. - Another and fuller discussion of the term *qūshbegī* see Bregel, *The Administration of Bukhara* , 7-12. Bregel comes to the conclusion that „throughout the reign of the Manghït dinasty [sic], from Muḥammad Raḥīm Khān to Amīr Naṣrallāh, *qoshbegi* was mentioned in contemporary sources as the highest official in Bukharan hierarchy“ (12). Bregel's study does not pretend to be the history of Bukharan administration just said to be a serious gap in the study of Central Asian history, but serves as a starting point. Bregel clearly shows the way: „A study of Bukharan administration requires the use of other sources [besides the *Majmaʿ al-arqām* and its sequel]. These are, in the first place, the decrees or diplomas of appointments; unfortunately, those of them that have survived are dispersed in various manuscript collections and mostly not even described and catalogued, let alone published.“ (19). - (Translator's note.)

watermarks of the Russian factory „Kummene", 18x11cm. This document is one of the rare examples in Central Asian documents where the corroboration is mentioned in the text; here, the imprint of the seal is mentioned by the expression *muhr namūdīm* „we sealed [it]", line 8. 420/337; two dates in the text, according to the Hijra and to the Christian calendars, both of them complete. 1336/1917, December.

In the group belonging to the period under study, there is a relatively large number of documents (more than 30 items) representing a special type of land lease. On the margins and on the verso of the sheets, contracts of lease concerning the same plots and the same persons are written, only at a higher rent. The renewal contracts are drawn up in an abbreviated form, the names of the lessees are not given, the plots not identified by size, quality or neighboring plots. Often, the date and the duration of the lease are not specified. The number of additional contracts written on each sheet together with the basic text varies from only one (464b/374, dated 1338/1920) to three (438b,v,g/354b,v,g, dated July 1920, but reflecting an even later contract). The rent to be paid in addition (*māzāda*) rose particularly sharply at the end of the period, in 1920, by up to 20% for one or two months.

Beneath every additional contract, the *qāḍī*'s seal was imprinted, but the traditional procedural formulae are missing, as e.g. the invocation, the names of the witnesses and other normally indispensable elements in private legal documents.[74] One such contract is published in Appendix II, number 5.

[74] It is well known that on September 19, 1924, the „Bukharan People's Soviet Republic" (Bukharskaia Narodnaia Sovetskaia Respublika BNSR) was newly dubbed „socialist", and thus, one „S" was added to the abbreviated form. See in A. Ishanov, *Bukharskaia Narodnaia Sovetskaia Respublika*. Tashkent 1969, 366.

4 *Documents from the early Soviet period (1920-26)*

Documents in the BOB collection dating from the period of the Bukharan Republic (BNSR and BNSSR, 1920-25) and the first years of the Uzbek SSR (1925-6) represent a smaller number of types than those from the preceding periods. Nevertheless, these late documents are also of considerable interest for historians and scholars specializing in diplomatics because of their particular features. Some of these features are as follows:

- These are documents representing the same types as their counterparts from the pre-colonial period. That is, they were issued according to the standard form of the late feudal period[75], but they are using new elements at the same time;
- the character of the officials' seals has changed. Whereas earlier, every official used his individual administrative seal, seals giving the administrative unit come into use now;
- new types of documents appear;
- the language used in the documents is changing, at least in part. Whereas private documents issued on the territory of the Bukharan Republic were still written in Persian (the usual language for such documents in the preceding periods), official documents are from now on written in Uzbek.

The short overview given in the following is arranged in chronological order.

4.1 Documents dating from the Bukharan Republic. In all, 18 items, most of them representing traditional types.

4.1.1 *„Traditional" types*

[75] The „late feudal period" is a special term in Soviet historiography, used to denote the 16th through 19th centuries of Central Asian history. I prefer not to change this term even if it is quite obviously a misnomer, but the question of „feudalism" in societies outside medieval Western Europe cannot be discussed in this place. (Translator's note.)

4.1.1.1 Document renewing a lease contract concerning *waqf* property leased by two persons (names given in the original contract). Above the text, symbolic invocation. Date of the contract not given; the document is, however, datable on the basis of data given in the original contract. This contract was concluded in July 1920 for a period of 6 months; thus, the additional document was drawn up after the proclamation of the Bukharan Republic. - The contract itself is documented in abbreviated form. Dates of conclusion, many procedural formulae, names of witnesses and so on have been left out. Some essential points are not stated either, as for instance the names of lessor and lessee, the object leased - these sould be the most important details. Instead of all this, there is only a short remark: „On the conditions mentioned in detail in the original document (*waṯīqa*) which is renewed by this contract", this is a reference to another contract to be found on the same sheet; this contract in turn also is a renewal of a contract of lease, but the document has the complete *form*. - The additional contract was written on the right margin of the older contract, and it is confirmed by the same seal as its predecessor. Imprint not fully legible, rather blurred, oval, 39x46mm, „Qāḍī mullā ʿIẓām ad-Dīn ṣadr raʾīs b. mullā Muḥammad ʿĀrif ṣadr muftī", dated 1335. - Factory-made paper, light ochre, 22x17cm. 5 lines of text. Irregular *nastaʿlīq* hand, black ink. 431b/348b. No date given (beginning of 1921).[76]

4.1.1.2 Copy of a purchase deed over half an orchard and half a house, drawn up on behalf of a woman (name, father's name and place of residence specified). - The document was drawn up in full compliance with the rules valid for deeds of sale from the late feudal period. The new elements concern some details: two dates given (according to the Hijra and Christian calendars), the *qāḍī*'s court has received a new name and the currency is another one. The main difference, however, is in the seal. A new type of seal is used here, it is a seal representing the office, not a person. It shows the coat of arms of the new state together with its name, it also identifies the

[76] For a contract of this type together with its addition, see the slightly earlier piece published in Appendix 2, number 5.

qāḍī's court. The name of the *qāḍī*, his patronym and his official rank are written over the seal. The names of the two witnesses are written in the same hand as the main body of the text. A registration number was entered at the top right corner. Document written in Persian, 9 lines of text and two additional notes, small elegant *nastaʿlīq* with elements of *dīwānī*. Black ink. Factory-made paper, light ochre, 16x17cm. Defects: The lower edge of the sheet with the lower part of the seal and the bottom right corner torn off. 267/204, dated 1339/1921.

4.1.1.3 Another purchase deed (160/143, dated 1340/1922) was drawn up one year later in the same court as the preceding one. It starts with a kind of (handwritten) sign, the official name of the Bukharan Republic, and the number of the court district. - In the top right corner, a registration number. The name of the single witness beneath the text without the special introductory formula normally preceding such entries in late feudal private documents (present in the preceding document).

4.1.1.4 Court decisions dividing an inheritance. 3 items, issued 1921 (370/293), 1922 (493/408) and 1923 (478/393). All of them were written conforming to the form characterizing this type of document in the pre-Soviet period with only a few newly introduced exterior features. Some of these are as follows: In the 1921 document, the number of the court district, the abbreviation for the Bukharan Republic and the full date according to the European calendar were entered on the right margin on the level of the first lines. The invocation formula is written above first line. The name and rank of the *qāḍī* are not written over the seal as in the other documents, but to the right of the seal and in an elaborately drawn frame. Names of witnesses not given. - In the 1922 act, only the invocation formula and beneath it a registration number have been entered in the upper part of the right margin. The names of the witnesses are to be found at their usual place together with the habitual introductory formula. - The 1923 document does not have an invocation formula.

A significant innovation in the standard form of private juridicial documents in the early Soviet period was that a given quantity of fee stamps was glued in free spaces of the document as proof that the charges payable for the given operation had been paid. These stamps carry inscriptions in two languages, in Uzbek (*Davlat markasi*) and in Russian (*Гербовая марка*). Besides, they show the coat of arms of the Bukharan Republic in their upper half and the abbreviation of its name beneath. Their value is indicated also in two languages, *tiyin* and *kop* (*копеек*, kopecks). On the 1922 document just described (division of an inheritance), 5 stamps worth from 5 to 75 kopecks have been glued on the lower margin, and on its 1923 counterpart, 5 stamps on the right margin: 4 worth 5 kopecks each, and one worth 75 kopecks.

4.1.1.5 Certificate of indebtedness, term of repayment not specified. Names of contracting parties given, and also debtor's place of residence - Chahārbāgh-i khāṣṣa (western suburb of Bukhara). - It is perhaps of interest to note that this document was drawn up in a court serving particularly the suburbs. The office is called (in Persian): *dār al-qaḍā'-i aṭrāf-i shahr-i Bukhārā-yi sharīf*, the same denomination is to be found on the seal (in Uzbek): *Bukhārā shūrālār jumhūriyatīning aṭrāf-i shahr qāḍīsī*. The name of the *qāḍī* was written over the seal with different ink and in another, irregular hand. - On this document, a stamp of the described type, value 5 kopecks. - Circular seal, 43mm, impressed at the usual spot. The formula indicating the presence of witnesses is extant, but their names are not given. This feature is quite frequently found in documents from the colonial period as has been stated above. - Above the main body of the text, a symbolic invocation. Text written in Persian, 7 lines, *dīwānī* script. Black ink. Factory-made yellowish paper, inferior quality. 21x15,5cm. 64/34, dated 1341/1922 (both dates given in text).

4.1.1.6 Act (*shahādat-nāma*) taken of the depositions made by three witnesses (names and patronyms given) concerning the true local position of three shops on some *waqf* ground (position and borders specified), and also the fact that the lessors of these shops have paid the due rents directly to some persons who receive material support by the endowment. This document shows a number of particular features. First, the date is not given at the beginning of the text (as was the rule in juridicial documents during the colonial period), but after the enumeration of the objects concerned (here, the shops). Further, a quite particular formula of procedure is introduced; we have not seen its identical equivalent in any of the documents known to us. At the end of the text, before the corroborative part attesting that the present document had been publicly transacted, we read: „On the strength of this, the information deposed by the witnesses has been laid down in a written act (*shahādat-nāma*) by the *qāḍī* of the second district of Bukhara" (lines 14-5). The closing formulae are however identical with those used in analogous documents from the late feudal period. - On this document, as on the other documents from the early Soviet period, stamps have been glued as proof of payment of the fees. One of these stamps, however, is not a *gerbovaia marka* in the true sense of this word, that is, it does not show the coat of arms of the Bukharan Republic, but the front façade of the Bukharan citadel, the Ark. The inscriptions are in Uzbek only and written in a very untrained hand. - Text in Persian, 15 lines, and 4 lines of notes in Uzbek concerning the registration of the document. Factory-made paper (of pre-revolutionary Russian produc-tion), ochre, 30x20cm. - To this document, a handwritten receipt has been glued, giving proof that the imam of the mosque mentioned in the main document has paid the government taxes. Text in Uzbek, 4 lines. Same seal and signature of *qāḍī*. Factory-made paper of inferior quality, 12x11cm. 457/372, dated 1343/1924.

4.1.1.7 Permit of the *qāḍī* handed out to the imam of the neighborhood mosque to conclude a marriage. In contrast to such acts dating from the pre-Soviet period, in this document, the age of the girl is stated directly - she is at least 15 years of age. - Above the text, official remarks: to the right, the abbreviation of the BNSR, to the left, the registration number. - Date given at the end of the document according to the European calendar. - Text in Uzbek, 4 lines. Seal and signature of *qāḍī* as in other BNSR documents. - Untrained *nastaʿlīq* hand, black ink. Factory-made paper, inferior quality. 16x17cm, December 1920.

4.1.2 *New types of documents*

4.1.2.1 Act (*shahādat-nāma*) drawn up by the examination board (*hai'at-i imtiḥān*) of the Religious Department of the Waqf Administration[77] giving proof that some Bukharan (name and patronym given) has passed the examination required for the office of imam at a neighborhood mosque, and that he has received the right (*istiḥqāq*) to act in the mentioned office. At the top of the document, its denomination is written - *shahādat-nāma*. Text in Uzbek, 5, 2 and 4 lines. The seal of the Waqf Administration beneath the text to the left. Date given according to the Hijra and the Christian calendars. Registration number to the right. Written in untrained *nasta'līq*, black ink. Factory-made yellowish paper. 12x22cm, 476/391, dated 1340/1922.

4.1.2.2 Letters (*chaqiruv khaṭṭ*) written to the district judges of Bukhara city attesting payment of the dues collected for orphans (*ṣaghīrlār āqchasī*) and receipts of corresponding documents. 5 items, all of them drawn up in December 1924, attested by the seal and signature of the *qāḍī* of the first district. Texts in Uzbek, written in a fixed form, 6 or 7 lines of text. Denomination of document written at top of sheet. A seal showing the arms of the Bukharan Republic impressed beneath the text in violet ink. Signatures of *qāḍī*s written either over the seal or to its right together with an abbreviated designation of office: „*Qāḍī* of the first [district]" or a fuller form: „People's *qāḍī* of the first [district]". - Written in irregular *nasta'līq*, black ink. Factory-made paper, 3 items ochre, 2 items light brown, one format: 11x12cm. 2a/128a; 3a/83a; 4a/82a; 5a/81a; 6a/15a.

4.1.2.3 Receipts attesting payment of the dues collected for orphans (*ṣaghīr naqdasī*), 3 items. Two documents show names of supported orphans. Documents drawn up according to a standard form. Above main body of text, denomination of

---

[77] *Религиозный отдел Управления Вакфов* in Russian. Corresponding documents from Samarqand have *Markaz auqāf idārasīnining dīnīya shu'basī* in Uzbek, and the impression of the seal reads *Б.Н.С.Р.Вакуфный отдел*, with the Uzbek form in the field: Abbreviation for the Bukharan People's Soviet Republic „B.Kh.Sh.J/M.N./ Markazī auqāf shu'basī". - We thank Florian Schwarz for the reference to the Samarqand documents. - (Translator's note.)

document: *kaftansa*, also at top: date according to Christian calendar to the left, registration number to the right. Main body of text in Uzbek, mentioning the fact that the dues had been paid, the sums received, name and patronym of taxpayer, amount of tax taken in to the benefit of a given orphan. - Beneath the text, signatures with designation of office, to the left border, half imprint of seals „People's *naẓīrat* (ministery, commissariat) of Justice", legends in Uzbek and Russian. (The other half of the imprint probably was on the receipt handed out to the taxpayer). - Texts in Uzbek, 4 lines each, written in irregular *nasta'līq*. Ink: dark red in two cases, green in the third. Factory-made paper, one format: 14x12cm. All documents dated 1924, earliest: January 12, latest: September 6. 55a/196a; 56a/192a; 84a/191a.

4.1.2.4 Declaration that a plot of land was taken over by a certain Ẓarīf b. Sharīf from two women (names given). In its outward appearance as well as in its inner structure, this document differs from analogous documents from the pre-Soviet as well as BNSR periods by its primitiveness and extreme lack of professionalism. The handwriting is informal to such a degree that many words cannot be deciphered. - The text in itself is a plain and short constatation of the transaction, a plot of land against a sum of money. No formalities were taken into account. Even the date was written in a totally whimsical manner. - Beneath the main text, the amounts of two taxes (given in *tiyin*) are stated (the names of the taxes can not be read). Beneath that, in the middle of the sheet, designation of office and signature of *qāḍī* (name not given); the signature is the same as in the acts described at 4.2.1. - The date is written above the first line, from right to left, without intervals, day and month, and year according to European calendar. - No seal. Text in Uzbek, 3 lines. Handwriting: „no style". Ink: between grey and brown. Factory-made paper, light brown. 11,5x11cm, 0/408, dated January 24, 1925.

4.1.2.5 Act about repayment of a debt to the creditor, the Ẓarīf b. Sharīf mentioned above, on behalf of two women (names given), both of them mentioned above in the description of the deed of sale. These women might be the executors of the estate of the deceased qārī Faiḍallāh who was the original debtor to Ẓarīf b. Sharīf. - The structure of this document again is peculiar. It starts without invocation with the description of the object given as payment for the debt, the plot of land mentioned above. Usually, lawsuits or *qāḍī* documents concerning the division of an inheritance begin like that. After that, the date (according to the two calendars), names of the parties, designation of the court district, and attestation that the plot of land has passed into the property of the plaintiff as a result of his suit. - The remaining formulae are written according to the late feudal standard pattern. - It is very hard to tell to which administrative or political unit this document belongs: the legends on the seal confirming the transaction are ambiguous. They seem to suggest that the seal served as the official symbol of the BNSR and the UzSSR at the same time. The legends in the outer circle (in Russian) and in the inner circle (in Uzbek) of the seal have the same meaning: „U.S.S.R. *Qāḍī* of the first district in Zeravshan province. Old Bukhara“[78]. In the center, however, the symbols of the BNSR can be seen: Above two crossed sheaves of ears and a sickle (in its Russian form), the abbreviation of the BNSR is quite clearly to be read (in Arabic letters), and beneath the abbreviation, the year 1343 is given (1924/5)[79]. - The *qāḍī*'s court is identified in the text as well, in the form *dār al-qaḍā'-i bīrinchī-yi Bukhārā-yi sharīf.* This is the same court where the deed of sale mentioned above (0/408) was drawn up as well as all other documents extant from the BNSR period in the BOB collection. The name of the *qāḍī* was written over the seal without specifying his rank in different ink and in another (but also irregular) hand. On the verso, a stamp glued to the document stating payment of government dues. - Text written in Persian, 9 lines of main text, 2 remarks (2 lines and 1 line). *Dīwānī*, black ink. Factory-made paper, ochre, pre-revolutionary Russian production. 22x17cm. 79/20, dated 1343/January 1925.

[78] *УССР Кази первого участка Зеравшанской долины. Старая Бухара* in Russian. Translator's note.

[79] The BNSR was renamed „socialist“ on September 19, 1924.

4.2 Documents from the first years of the Uzbek SSR (1925-6)

This is a small group containing only 9 items, all of them drawn up in the city of Bukhara (Old Bukhara) which was then the administrative center of Zeravshan province, USSR (this abbreviation - USSR - was used for the Uzbek SSR on the seals of the documents extant from this period).[80]

The documents in this group show a number of peculiarities which may be of interest. They are all written in the style of private legal documents dating from the late feudal period. All documents but one (stemming from Vabkent, 1926) are written in Persian. The seals are impressed with ink, and they (all identical) carry the following legends signifying two political units: USSR (in cyrillic script, on the outer ring) for the Uzbek SSR, and BIShJ[81] (in Arabic script, on the inner ring) for the Bukharan Socialist Soviet Republic.

In this group, the majority of documents is about the legal division of inheritance and about the execution of this decision: handing over the parts to the heirs. The following type of document recurs several times:

4.2.1 Waiver of a part of an inheritance against compensation. In the corroborative part, the customary formula introducing the names of the witnesses is included. The number of witnesses, however, is somewhat surprising: Ten names are given. - This document type displays some new features: Above the right margin, two registration numbers. Beneath the text, a seal of the new „government" type, in two languages as described above. Name of the *qāḍī* written over the seal imprint. - Main body of text in Persian, designation of court in Uzbek. 7 lines of text (plus two remarks, 1 line and 2 lines). *Nastaʿlīq*. Ink: black in main body of text, name of *qāḍī* and registration numbers - between grey and brown. Russian pre-revolutionary paper, 22x17cm. 68a/30a, dated 1343/April 1925 (both dates given in text). To the document, a receipt attesting payment of government dues has been glued, names and amount of dues specified. Registration number 68b/30b, dated April 7, 1925.

[80] The abbreviation USSR was later on used for the Ukrainian SSR. - (Translator's note.)

4.2.2 *Qāḍī*'s decision dividing up an inheritance. Names of heirs and degree of relation given. Document drawn up in accordance with the standard form of the late feudal period. Text in Persian, 10+1+1+1 lines. Fine *nasta'līq*. Seal (beneath text) of the type discussed above. Ink: as in preceding document. Russian pre-revolutionary paper. 386/308, dated 1343/April 1925. On the right margin, fee stamps of the USSR have been glued, attesting that government dues have been paid. - Two more documents of the same type and in the same standard form: 351/274, dated 1343/April 1925, and 388/310, dated 1343/May 1925.

4.2.3 Receipt of an agent (guardian) having received the parts of an inheritance due to the minors on whose behalf he is acting (all names given). The form of the given document is identical to those from the late feudal period. On top, symbolic invocation. Seals of the type discussed above. Text written in Persian, 8+1+1+1 lines. *Nasta'līq*. Ink: Text written in black ink, imprints of seals: violet ink. Russian pre-revolutionary paper. No fee stamps. 66/32, dated 1343/January 1926. - To the document, a receipt attesting payment of government dues has been stitched. Text in Uzbek, irregular hand, same date as main document.

4.2.4 Act of withdrawal of lawsuit. Taken upon public declaration of plaintiff that he has no claims against the defendant (names given). Drawn up according to the typical standard form of the late feudal period. Text written in Persian, 6+1+2 lines plus the names of the witnesses. Seal of the mentioned type. Function and signature of *qāḍī* over the seal. Fine and elegant *nasta'līq*. Black ink. Russian pre-revolutionary paper, 22x17cm. 63/35, dated 1343/April 1925. - To the document, a receipt attesting payment of government dues has been glued. Text in Uzbek, very irregular hand, 1343/May 1925.

4.2.5 *Qāḍī*'s decision handing over derelicts. The documents consists of two parts. First, a fiduciary (*qaiyim*) for the absent owner of the goods is named (names given). Second, the goods are handed over to this fiduciary who also has the right

[81] *Bukhārā ishtirākī shūrālār jumhūrīyatī.*

to keep and work with the ready money belonging to the absent owner until he shows up again. - Text written in Persian, 8 lines. No witnesses named. Seal of discussed type. Careless *nastaʿlīq*. Black ink. Russian pre-revolu-tionary paper, 21x16cm. 65/33, dated 1343/September 1925.

4.2.6 Letter of power of attorney (*wakālat ḫaṭṭ*). *Qāḍī* bears witness that he has named an attorney to act for a certain woman, enabling this man to receive from the orphanage goods and money belonging to a minor boy and to hand these goods over to the woman. - Text written in Persian, 9+1+1 lines. No invocation. Seal of the BNSR. Irregular *nastaʿlīq*. Russian pre-revolutionary paper, 21x14cm. 477/392, dated February 1926/1344 (like this in the text, the European date coming first). - To the document, a receipt attesting payment of government dues has been stitched with a needle. Text in Uzbek, written in careless tall *nastaʿlīq*. Factory-made paper, 11,5x11cm, dated 1926 (Hijra date not given).

The descriptions given for this latest group of documents (1920-6) are hoped to be of interest not only for scholars of diplomatics in a narrow sense, but also for social historians and those interested in the evolution of government and other institutions and the judiciary as a whole in the BNSR and the first years of the Uzbek SSR.

Topography of chanceries

The term *chancery* will be employed here not in its narrow sense as an office in the central administration responsible for drawing up the necessary documentation, but in a broader sense as any office or place where within the context of late feudal Central Asia different kinds of documents were written and issued.

The first group of chanceries, then, consists of the amir's court and other central government offices, for instance, the office of the Chief scribe (*munshī*), where grants (land grants and others), decrees, orders and letters (official and private ones) were written on behalf of the khan or amir, the offices of the various high officials residing in the capital: the office of the head of the civilian administration (or the head of the government), the head of the tax department, the head of the military department, the various departments serving the palace, the office of the supreme *qāḍī* and the supreme jurisconsult (*aʿlam*), and also the administrations responsible for the capital city, as for instance the city *qāḍī*, the *muḥtasib* and the *raʾīs*.

The second group includes the chanceries of provincial and *tūmān* officials, governors, *raʾīs*es, *qāḍīs*, tax collectors, water administrators (*mīrāb*) and so on.

The third group of chanceries is made up of scribal „offices" active wherever private persons could have a petition or demand, a lawsuit or simply a letter written in the customary form. This work could be done by scribes otherwise active in the *qāḍī*'s or *muftī*'s office, or by any person well-versed in the scribal arts, working at home or in a madrasa.

And finally, a „chancery" is, within the context of this paper, defined as the place where a document was written. This designation is chosen whenever it turned out to be impossible to establish which chancery has issued the document, either directly from the text or indirectly on the basis of seals, the contents, paleographic clues and so forth.

The documents in the BOB collection originate from a wide variety of chanceries situated all over the Bukharan khanate/amirate and also beyond its borders. These places are directly identified in only one group of documents, those concerning private business. For another one - the *qāḍī* document - the name of the office and its district can easily be established by the seals, by geographical names mentioned in the text and so on. Further, there is no difficulty with documents written in the khan's or amir's chancery. It is, however, not always easy to find out at what particular place the document was written, since there are cases of documents being issued by the ruler when he was away from the capital.

It is much more difficult to establish where and in which chancery documents issued by local administrators were written. If at all possible, this has to be deducted from indirect evidence, as for instance placenames or historical persons mentioned in the text. Sometimes the last resort is to draw an analogy to other documents which can be connected to a given local chancery beyond doubt.

The most problematic group of documents in this respect are „incoming" letters and petitions, that is, letters addressed by private persons to officials, as well as ordinary business correspondence, accounts and so forth; often, these cannot be located at all.

The majority of the documents in the BOB collection were written either in the city of Bukhara itself or else in the *tūmān*s of Bukhara province.

1. The city of Bukhara

More than half the documents in the BOB collection were written in the various chanceries active in the city of Bukhara (more than 400 items). The oldest document in the collection, the endowment deed in favor of the shrine of Saif ʿad-dīn Bākharzī (see above), was issued by the Bukharan *qāḍī*'s office as evident from the following entry among the witnesses: „This was written by Abū l-Ḥamd Muḥammad [...] qāḍī and shaikh al-islām of the city of Bukhara and its environs [name added]".[82]

In another document - the earliest among Central Asian documents to have come down to us not in literary form, as an insertion into narrative or legal literature, but as a separate document, an endowment deed from the end of the 13th century[83], the place of the chancery is likewise to be identified on the basis of indirect evidence: „the supreme judge, the head of judges [...], Abū l-Faḍl Muḥammad b. Muḥammad al-Bukhārī, leading the judiciary in the district [*kūra*] of Bukhara and its environs, [says:] I state the exactness and legal soundness of this endowment, its being permitted [by the Sharia] and its validity. [...] On the strength of all this, I announce the following decision [...] and sign the decision. Transacted in the *qāḍī*'s court in the *kūra*".[84] Since *kūra* is used for the city of Bukhara in the middle of the *sijill* as well as at its end, it is clear that the chancery was the *qāḍī*'s court in that city where the court of the supreme judge was located.

The documents written in Bukhara originate from the following chanceries.

1.1 The *qāḍī*'s court. In some cases, the *qāḍī*'s court of the city of Bukhara is mentioned in the text, as for instance in the following form: *dār al-qaḍā-yi balda-yi fākhira-yi Bukhārā-yi sharīf*. This holds for about 100 items in the collection (162/145, dated 1231/1816, and 42/49, dated 1337/1919, to name but two out of this number). In other cases, the seal of the supreme judge was impressed beneath the text of the document, which in itself is a hint at the document's having been drawn up in Bukhara (577/479, dated 1222/1808; 131/182, dated 1316/1898; 437/353, dated 1338/1920).

[82] O.D. Chekhovich, *Bukharskie dokumenty XIV v*, 111 (text), 186 (Russian text), 317-8 (facsimile), line 951 of published text.

[83] The document is extant in a copy dated from the end of the 13th century (in the original Arabic) and a Persian translation dating from the end of the 18th century. - See *Bukharskii vakf*, Introduction, p. 30 and 35.

[84] *Bukharskii vakf XIII v.* Moskva 1979, 58-60 (text), 77-8 (Russian translation). Lines 239-62, the Persian translation of the *sijill*.

1.2 Chancery of the *ra'īs*. Some documents were drawn up at the chancery of the Bukharan *ra'īs* (about 170 items, none of them dated earlier than the 1870s). There seem to be no typological differences between these documents and those issued at the *qāḍī*'s court. In other words, both offices were competent to prepare the same types of notarial acts, and any division of competence as may have existed was, at any rate, without effect upon the types of documents issued. - Fifty years ago, O.D. Chekhovich, the leading specialist in the field of Bukharan historical documents, drew scholarly attention to the fact that two offices existed in pre-Soviet Bukhara as offices of notary. She established that in the second half of the 19th century, private documents concerning the suburbs and agricultural districts surrounding Bukhara „were recorded in the chancery of the Bukharan *ra'īs* (*dār al-iḥtisāb*). Until then, all these documents had been recorded by the supreme *qāḍī* (*qāḍī-kalān*) [...]. As the number of transactions increased, the right to record them was conferred upon both the *qāḍī-kalān* and the *ra'īs*."[85] Thus, the division of labor between the *qāḍī* and the *ra'īs* followed territorial lines. A brief remark about the chancery of the *ra'īs* seems to be in order here. This was called *dār al-iḥtisāb*, which literally means „chancery/office of the *muḥtasib*" who was in charge of controlling the markets and watching over public morals. This official was called *ra'īs* in late 19th-early 20th century Bukhara.[86] About 80 private juridicial documents mention the office or chancery of the *ra'īs-muḥtasib* in the text (*dār al-iḥtisāb-i balda-yi fākhira-yi Bukhārā-yi sharīf*), e.g. 159/142, dated 1294/1877; 436/352, dated 1337/1919. 80 more

[85] O.D. Chekhovich, „Ob aktovykh materialakh po istorii Bukhary". - In: *Istoricheskie zapiski* t. 16, Moskva 1945, 236.

[86] Mīrzā Badī'-dīvān, *Majma' al-arqām*. Moskva 1981, 115 (editor's glossary, A.B. Vil'danova). (The term *ra'īs* is one of the most multi-faceted ones in medieval and early modern Islamic history. Its basic meaning is „head of a given group"; this group can be a school of law, a neighborhood of a town, a guild of craftsmen and so forth. In some cases, the term comes close to signify a person in charge of public affairs in a given city, of establishing peace within the city walls and dealing with outside partners or enemies, including the ruler to whose dominion the town belongs. There is a large body of literature on this subject, see the corresponding article in *EI²* (A. Havemann). The question of how cities and rulers interacted in early modern Central Asia is still awaiting an in-depth study. - Translator's note.)

documents show the imprint of the seal of the *ra'īs*, among them 43/48, dated 1279/1862; 30/60, dated 1338/1920.

1.3 The chancery at the amir's court was naturally another place in Bukhara where documents were issued. There are about sixty of them in the BOB collection. It has to be noted that in Central Asian rulers' documents, the place where the document was issued is not normally mentioned. The chancery can thus only be identified on indirect evidence, by its contents or by the seals of the ruler or court officials.

1.3.1 Documents issued on behalf of the khan/amir:

1.3.1.1 Purchase deed and partial exemption from taxes of government land, transacted by a person acting as attorney (name given) on behalf of Subḥān-Qūlī Khān, 570/477, dated 1108/1697 (see above, text at note 29),

1.3.1.2 Decree issued by amir Naṣrallāh confirming a grant conferred by the preceding ruler, 295/225, dated 1242/1827

1.3.2 Documents not mentioning the name of the ruler. In these cases, the ruler can be identified by the date:

1.3.2.1 Decree by Abū l-Faiḍ Khān confirming a subject in his ownership rights, 296/226, dated 1130/1717-8,

1.3.2.2 Decree by amir ʿĀlim addressed to the supreme *qāḍī*, 307/237, dated 1337/1919.

1.4 Chanceries of the highest official jurists. The chancery is not given by name, but established on the basis of the jurists' seal.

1.4.1 *Fatwā* attested by the seal of the *aʿlam* (highest jurisconsult[87]), 142/125, dated not before 1248/1832-3 (dated by the seal),

1.4.2 *Fatwā* attested by the seal of the *ūrāgh*[88], 12a/75a, dated not before 1324/1906-7 (dated by the seal),

[87] The title is an abridged form for *muftī-yi aʿlam* and was used in this way. *Majmaʿ al-arqām*, fol. 87a. He was issuing *fatwās* to the population in contrast to his colleague, the *muftī-yi ʿaskar*, who was acting for the „military". - (Translator's note.)

[88] This official was acting as a *muḥtasib* among the saiyids in the „military". *Majmaʿ al-arqām*, fol. 87b. - (Translator's note.)

1.4.3 *Fatwā* issued in the name of the highest representative of the Shiite school of law (*ḥujjat al-islām*), 552/466, dated not before 1308/1890 (dated by the seal).

1.5 Documents issued by the chanceries of the BNSR. Most of the documents originating from the BNSR period were written in the city of Bukhara and a few more in the immediate vicinity of the city.

1.5.1 Five private documents drawn up at the *qāḍī*'s court in the city of Bukhara. The chancery is identified by the legend of the seal and once more by a note above the signature of the *qāḍī*. Two of them belong to the first court district, 370/293, dated 1339/1921 (division of inheritance). The three others belong to the second court district, among them the act taken of witness (*shahādat-nāma*), 457/372, dated 1924.

1.5.2 An official document certifying payment of government dues, 478/372, dated 1924.

1.6 Documents concerning Zeravshan province, UzSSR (1925-6), 17 items in all, in two types: private and official documents, the private documents drawn up in the court offices of the first and second court districts of Bukhara city, the official documents all being receipts (*ordir*) attesting payment of government dues (see above, chapter on documents from the early Soviet period).

2. Documents from chanceries in the suburbs and outskirts of Bukhara. 7 private documents.

2.1 *Qāḍī*'s court at Utrār (to the south-west of the city), e.g.: deed of sale, 110/93, dated 1278/1862.

2.2 „Southern" court, *janūbī-yi rūd-i Bukhārā-yi sharīf*, e.g.: certificate of indebtedness, 37/54, dated 1338/1920.

2.3 In the BNSR period, three documents now in the BOB collection were drawn up in a court chancery particularly designed to serve the outskirts of Bukhara. The chancery is identified in three different parts of the documents, in the main text: „*Qāḍī*'s court for the outskirts of Bukhara the Noble" (*dār al-qaḍā-yi aṭrāf-i Bukhārā-yi sharīf*), in the legend of the seal (in Uzbek): „*Qāḍī* for the outskirts of

Bukhara, Bukharan Soviet Republic" (*Bukhārā shūrālār jumhūriyatīning aṭrāf-i shahar qaḍīsī*), and third, beneath the text, before the signature of the *qāḍī*: „People's judge of the outskirts" (in Uzbek: *aṭrāf khalq qāḍīsī*). For instance, certificate of indebtedness, 64/34, dated 1341/1922.I

3. Chanceries in the *tūmāns* of Bukhara province.

More than 10 documents were drawn up in chanceries working in various *tūmāns* of Bukhara province. In some of the texts, the chancery is mentioned, in others, it can unequivocally be identified by the contents.

3.1 *Tūmān* Kām-i Abū Muslim, 5 items. Examples: Purchase deed, court (*dār al-qaḍā*) mentioned in text, 435/351, dated 1281/1872; private letter, chancery identified by contents, 531/445, dated 1336/1917-8.

3.2 *Tūmān* Sāmījān (present-day district (*tuman*) of Romitan), 3 items. In two documents, the chancery is mentioned (according to the standard pattern); e.g., confirmation of a grant issued by order of the khan by the *tūmān* governor. The third document is classified here for its contents.

3.3 *Tūmān* Khairābād (partly corresponding to the present-day district (*tuman*) of Jondor), 3 items, e.g. certificate of indebtedness, 86/13, dated 1328/1910.

3.4 Some documents were drawn up in *tūmān* Kāmāt, e.g., registration numbers 435/351, dated 1289/1872, deed of sale, chancery mentioned in the text. - Those documents should be classified with the group in which the court chancery at Vābkant is mentioned. 2 items: A letter of power of attorney (*wakālat khaṭṭ*), the location of the court chancery is given at three places: in the text according to the standard pattern, beneath the text, before the *qāḍī*'s signature, and on the legend of the seal. 477/392a, dated 1926/1344 (with the European date coming first). The second document is a receipt attesting payment of govern-ment dues. Again, the place of the chancery is given in three variants, beneath the text, before the *qāḍī*'s signature, and twice on the seal (in the Russian and the Uzbek parts). 477b/392b, dated 1926 (like this in the text, European date only).

4. Chanceries in the provinces of the Bukharan amirate.

In some cases, the chancery is mentioned in the text, and in others, it can be identified by the contents.

4.1 Ḍiyā ad-Dīn province, 10 private documents, drawn up in the *qāḍī*'s court in 1906-7.

4.2 Karmīna province, 3 items:

4.2.1 Purchase deed, court mentioned in text according to standard form, 41/50, dated 1286/1870,

4.2.2 Two private letters written towards the end of the 19th or at the beginning of the 20th century.

4.3 Qarshī province, 3 items, written on the recto and verso of one sheet.

4.3.1 Lawsuit pursued from Qarshī (judging by the contents), not dated.

4.3.2 Withdrawal of lawsuit, registered at the *qāḍī*'s court, dated 1326/1908 on the verso of the sheet.

4.3.3 Document written on the verso of this sheet, above the act of withdrawal, an order of the amir to the *qāḍī* (officiating in Qarshī province), written in Bukhara in 1324/1906-7. Common registration number 135/118.

4.4 Nasaf province. This was the name more commonly used for Qarshī province since the second half of the 19th century. 37 items. In 11 of them, the *qāḍī*'s court of this province is referred to. In all probability, this court was located in the town of Nasaf, e.g., 51/11, dated 1287/1870. In two other private documents, the place is given as the court at Jūy-i naw, Nasaf province, e.g. 35/36, dated 1313/1896. The remaining documents have been located by their contents or by comparison of their seals.

4.5 City of Samarqand. 3 items. In the case of two deeds of sale, the *qāḍī*'s court is mentioned, 17/3, dated 1116/1704; 178/495, dated 1126/1714. In the case of the decree issued by Nawrūz Aḥmad Khān (the Shibanid ruler), Samarqand has been assumed to be the place of issue since this city was the center of his appanage, 16/6, dated 963/1556.

4.6 In the text of one document - a receipt - the chancery is called *dār al-qaḍā'-i wilāyat-i Khuzār*, „*qāḍī*'s court of Khuzār province". This is present-day Guzor east of Qarshī/Nasaf. 35/56, dated 1313/1896.

4.7 In the text of three documents, the chancery is called „*Qāḍī*'s court of Shahrisabz province". Taking into account that Shahrisabz (as well as Khuzār, mentioned above) was an insignificant town in the Kashka-Darya valley in the late feudal period, it is possible that the term *wilāyat* does not mean a province in this case, but a *tūmān* which then would probably have belonged to Qarshi/Nasaf province. One of the documents is the *waqf* endowment 14/73, dated 1315/1898.[89]

4.8 *Qāḍī* court of Chahārjūy province, mentioned in four documents drawn up between 1910 and 1914. - The town of Chārjūy can be identified without doubt as the place where a private letter was written (datable to end of 19th-beginning of 20th century).

4.9 In the BOB collection, there are the following documents written at other places within the Bukharan amirate:

4.9.1 Baisūn, situated in present-day Surkhandar'inskaia oblast', Uzbekistan. Pawn ticket, 501/416, datable to the 19th century.

4.9.2 Kerki, situated in present-day Turkmenistan, accompanying letter, 498/413, dated 1338/1919/1920.

4.9.3 Kitāb, situated in present-day Kashkadar'inskaia oblast', Uzbekistan. Purchase deed with defect text, 7/4, datable to the end of the 19th century.

For more than 250 documents, the place of origin could not be ascertained. But most of them were certainly issued within the borders of the Bukharan amirate.

[89] The administrative history of the Bukharan amirate in the 19th century has yet to be written. In my opinion, the hints in the documents should be taken more seriously. It is well established that Shahrisabz was a rather independent unit during much of the 18th and 19th centuries, heavily contested, and the town cannot simply be dismissed as an insignificant place. It cannot even be seen as yet another part of the Bukharan emirate. - (Translator's note.)

5. Documents written abroad (outside the Bukharan amirate)

In the BOB collection, there are more than forty various documents written outside the Bukharan amirate, or in residences of foreign ambassadors or of other representatives in Bukhara. They were written between the end of the 18th century and the establishment of Soviet power.

5.1 The earliest of these documents is a purchase deed written in Najaf (Iraq), 540/454, dated 1203/1789.

5.2 One letter was written in Khiva to a certain Bukharan jurist (name not given), asking him to explain some legal question, 226/165, dated 1338/1919.

5.3 Most of the letters in this group come from Afghanistan. Two letters (datable to end of 19th-beginning of 20th century) were written in Kabul (520/435). Three private legal documents drawn up in Shiburghān, dated 1914 and 1915 (398/315, dated 1332/1914). One document from Ṭāliqān (399/316, dated 1333/1915). The following *qāḍī* documents are worth mentioning: protocol confirming rights to a inheritance (318/247, dated 1329/1911); three acts attesting that property had been received after the death of Afghan subjects who had died in Bukhara (397/314, dated 1333/1915); a copy of the lithographed proclamation of the Afghan amir Ḥabībullāh (211/150a, dated 1324/1906, name of amir read on seal). To the group of „Afghan" documents the diplomatic letters written by the Afghan ambassador in Bukhara can be added, 515/430, dated 1337/1919.

5.4 In the BOB collection, four letters written home by Bukharan pilgrims (from Medina) are preserved, dating from 1893-7. These are all in Arabic. One of them was written by three brothers (as evident from the seals on the verso) to the amir of Bukhara (identified by the formula used for address), registration number 315/244, two seals dated 1308/1890-1; another was written by one of the brothers (going by the seal) to the supreme judge of Bukhara (again, identified by the formula used for address, names not mentioned), registratioin number 316, dated 1308/1890-1 (by the seal), this one is in Arabic verses.

5.5 Other countries where documents in the BOB collection originated include (Ottoman) Turkey, India, Xinjiang (Yārkand in particular) and others.

5.6 Documents of Russian origin include a petition drawn up by a notary in Moscow (in Russian, 156b/139b, dated November 15, 1917) and two receipts handed out by the Russian representative in New Bukhara (Kagan) in 1894, in Russian, 33a/8a and 33b/8b.

To sum up the results of the chronological and topographical description of the BOB collection, it contains nearly 700 items spanning a long period, 600 years of Bukharan history, from the endowment deed in favor of the shrine of Saif ad-dīn Bākharzī (1326) to the papers written in 1926, Zeravshan province, UzSSR. In terms of geographical distribution as well, the collection covers a wide area. Even if its essential parts pertain to the city of Bukhara and the lower Zeravshan valley, a significant portion stems from other parts of present-day Uzbekistan, especially the Kashkadarya valley. Other parts of present-day Uzbekistan are also represented, if only by a single document or very small numbers, and samples from the rest of the Muslim world attest wider contacts through trade and pilgrimage. Perhaps the most important feature of the collection is that it contains almost all types of documents, issued by rulers and *qāḍīs*, drawn up by private persons in connection with business as well as private affairs.

APPENDIX I

Short Glossary of terms used in the documents

Abbreviations: a - Arabic, p - Persian, t - Turkī, r - Russian

aʿlam, a. Short for *muftī-yi aʿlam*, head *muftī*, in charge of giving juridicial responsa to the non-military civilian population.

amīn, a. Guardian of legal minors, appointed by the *qāḍī*, and authorized to represent his wards in all kinds of transactions.

arāḍī, a., sg. *arḍ* „land". Plots of land as objects of transactions, such as grants, sale and lease.

aṣālatan, a. Power of a transacting party to act in his own right, particularly if he is acting, in the same transaction, also for another party as attorney for somebody else (*aṣālatan wa-wakālatan*).

badal, a. Equivalent value given in return or in compensation in a private contract (as in a purchase), in most cases given in money.

baiʿ, a. Private contract of exchange; sale; has the two following forms.

baiʿ-i bātt or *baiʿ-i bātt-i batāt*, a-p. Contract of sale (irrevocable after conclusion apart from certain particular cases).

baiʿ-i jāʾiz, a-p. Mortgage (giving away landed property as security for a loan), literally „permitted sale".

banda nawāzā, p. „Oh you, who treat your slaves with clemency", formula used as address in letters to the rulers of 19th and early 20th century Bukhara.

chuhra-bāshī or *chuhra-āqāsī*, t. Military title.

dādkhwāh, p. Court official in charge of administering petitions and complaints. Also known to have had military functions.

dah-bāshī, p. Literally, „commander of ten". Military title.

dahdū, p. Land/produce tax, basically one fifth of produce (see *kharāj*).

dahyak, p. Tithe (see *'ushr*).

dār al-iḥtisāb, a. Office of the *muḥtasib*. In private documents, one of the two chanceries where notarial acts could be drawn up in late 19th- early 20th century Bukhara. This was the office of the *ra'īs* who acted as a notary besides his function as *muḥtasib*.

dār al-qaḍā', a. Court of justice. Main chancery for private documents.

dīwānbegī, p. Head of civilian administration, in particular taxation and treasury.

faḍīlat wa-faqāhat-panāh, a-p. „Refuge of excellence and jurisprudence", official title for *qāḍīs*..

farmān, p. Decree issued by a khan or amir.

ġabn, a. „deceit", used in the formula *bi-lā ġabn*,. „without deceit", used to affirm private contracts. Frequently also used as *bi-lā ġabn wa-lā ġurūr*, meaning the same thing.

guḏar, p. Neighborhood in a town or city.

ḥākim, a. Literally „decision maker", used in the formula *ḥākim-i shar'-i sharīf*, a-p, „who decides according to the noble law", address used for *qāḍīs*.

ḥāl jawāz iqrārihī shar'an, a. Formula used to indicate that the person making a legal deposition is legally entitled to depose, „when he was legally able to do so".

ḥisba, a. See *ra'īs*.

ḥuḍḍār, a. „Persons present", witnesses, as in the formula *ḥuḍḍār al-majlis*, witnesses of the transaction. This formula is often scrawled in a nearly illegible form as a shorthand note in a stylized form.

ḥujjat al-islām, a. „Proof of Islam", title used for Shiite jurists and *'ulamā'*.

ḥukm, a. Decision, decree issued by a ruler, as in the *intitulatio* formulae *ḥukm-i ʿālī shud* or *ḥukm-i jahān-muṭāʿ shud*, a-p.

ibrāʾ, a. Acquittance or waiver of a claim, used in the formula *ibrāʾ namūdam*, a-p, in withdrawals of a suit against a debtor. The acts are therefore called *khaṭṭ-i ibrāʾ*.

iḥtisāb, a. See *raʾīs* and *dār al-iḥtisāb*.

ijāra, a. Contract of lease (tenancy).

imām, a. Person leading the daily prayers. Can be appointed in an endowment deed.

ʿināyat-nāma, a-p. Deed taken of a grant.

iqrār, a. Public acknowledgement, declaration or deposition made by the vendor in deeds of sale (or in analogous cases, by the acting party).

jūy, p. Irrigation canal.

jūy-i ʿāmm, public irrigation canal, or canal owned by a plurality of people, such as a village or a city neighborhood, and *jūy-i khāṣṣ*, private canal.

kaftansa, r. Corrupted Russian, correct form *kvitantsiia*, „receipt".

kāna ḏālika, a. „This was [done, declared]", formula used to indicate that a declaration was made in public, usually introducing the witnesses, as in *wa-kāna ḏālika fī maḥḍar al-ṯiqāt*, „this was declared in the presence of the [following] trustworthy people".

kharāj, a. Land/produce tax which in Central Asia eventually came to mean basically „one fifth of produce or its value in money".

khaṭṭ, a. Writing, term used for any kind of private document, such as *khaṭṭ-i nikāḥ* (contract of marriage), *khaṭṭ-i ibrāʾ* (withdrawal of a lawsuit) and so forth.

kūcha, p-t. Street in a town or city.

maḥḍar, a. „Presence", of witnesses, as used in the formula *bi-maḥḍar (min) al-ṯiqāt* (or other terms used for the witnesses), frequently found as corroboration in private documents.

maḥram, a. Literally „a close relative with whom marriage is not permitted", an intimate, also a court title.

majārī, pl. of *majrā*, a. Streams of water, irrigation canals.

mawḍiʿ, a. Rural settlement.

mazraʿa, a. Arable land of any size.

mīrākhūr, p. Chief equerry, title of a court official in charge of the ruler's stable.

muʿād, a. Literally „return". Term of recurrent payment in rentals and leases.

muʾaḏḏin, a. Person calling to prayer. Can be appointed in the clauses of an endowment deed.

mubārak-nāma, a-p. Decision of the ruler in (positive) response to a petition.

muftī, a. Scholar and/or official giving legal responsa.

muḥtasib, a. See *raʾīs*.

munshī, a. Scribe, clerk.

muqarr ʿalaihi, a. Person in whose favor a public declaration *iqrār* is given (e.g. the buyer *mushtarī* of an identified object in a deed of sale or the lessee *mustaʾjir* in a lease contract).

muqirr, a. Person giving a public declaration *iqrār* (e.g., that he has sold a identified object to a named person), the active part in a private contract of any sort.

musammāt, a. Literally „the named one (fem.)", introducing the name of a woman participating in a legal transaction.

mushāʿ, a., also *mushtarak(a)*, a. Property held jointly by two or more persons.

mushtarī, a. Buyer.

mustaʾjir, a. Lessee (tenant) in a lease contract.

mutawallī, a. Administrator of a *waqf*, normally named in the endowment deed.

muwakkil, a. Person empowering an attorney (*wakīl*) to act on his or her behalf in a legal transaction.

nāʾib, a. Deputy (e.g., of a *qāḍī*).

nikāḥ, a. Marriage, thence *khaṭṭ-i nikāḥ*, contract of marriage.

nishān, p. Decree, order, and one of the terms used to refer to them in the documents themselves.

ordir, r. Corrupted Russian, correct form *order*, „order".

qabūl, a. Acceptance, consent, as in the formula *ma'a qabūlihī* used to indicate that a given transaction was freely undertaken by the mentioned party.

qaraulbīgī, t. Military title. Officer in charge of internal security (roads).

qaṭ' karda ba-ijāra dāda shud, p. „It was detached and handed over in lease to", formula used in contracts of lease (tenancy).

qibla-gāh, a-p. „Place [acting as] *qibla*", formula used to address men older than the writer (in private and official letters).

qiṭ'a, a. Plot of land as object of a transaction.

qūshbīgī, t. Literally „head falconer", used for a high-ranking military commander. In late 19th-early 20th century Bukhara, head of executive power in the amirate.

rāh, p. Way. A street in a town or city, frequently mentioned as delimitation for the object of a legal transaction.

rāh-i 'āmm, p-a. Public thouroughfare.

ra'īs, a. In the late Bukharan amirate, term used for the person in charge of the *iḥtisāb* or *ḥisba*: control of public morale and good manners as well as weights and measures in the marketplace.

rūd, p. River, canal. *Rūd-i balda-yi Bukhārā*, term used for the very ancient main canal serving the city of Bukhara which still flows through the city center. Often used in documents as a topographical indicator for places in the city, but also in outlying districts. Also, name of one or two *tūmān*s.

ṣadr, a. Official in charge of supervising endowment (*waqf*) holdings situated in or close to the city of Bukhara.

sana, a. Year. The word is usually written in the documents with the initial letter *sīn* drawn out so that the year can be written over that line (in numbers).

shahādat-nāma, a-p. Act of witness/testimony given in court.

shāhid, a. Witness.

shahr, a. Month, introducing the name of the month in dating.

shart, a. Condition, terms, stipulations.. Used as a term in endowment deeds, *shart kard wāqif* (a-p), „The endower (I) stipulated as conditions [for this endowment]", introducing the various clauses of disposition; sometimes the formula is repeated before every single clause.

shart, a. Used also in private documents as a term of ensuring the validity of the contract, *bi-lā shart fāsid*, „without any unsound condition [endangering the unhampered validity of the contract]. See also *ġabn.*

ṣudūr, a. Official in charge of supervising endowment (*waqf*) holdings in the rural districts of the Bukharan oasis.

sukniyāt, a., also *uskuna.* Any kind of property produced by human labor on a given plot of land: plants, trees, buildings and so forth. Can form the object of a transaction separately from the land itself.

ṭalāq, a. Divorce (repudiation of a wife by her husband). Can also form the subject of a contract.

tanga, p-t. Coin, currency (mostly silver).

ta'rīkh, a. Date. Used to introduce the date in private documents.

taṣadduq, a. Sacrifice. Used in the formula (p) *taṣadduq-i sar-i mawlāyam shawam*, „Let me be the sacrifice offered for my master's head", used as address in letters written to the rulers in late 19th - early 20th century Bukhara.

taṣadduq, a. Charity. Used in the formula (p) *waqf kardam wa-taṣadduq-i shar'ī namūdam*, „I endowed as a *waqf* and made a legally acceptable charity".

ṯiqa, pl. *ṯiqāt*, a. Trustworthy person(s). Term used for introducing the witnesses, as in *kāna ḏālika fī maḥḍar al-ṯiqāt* (see).

tūmān, t. Territorial administrative unit. Several *tūmān* make up one *wilāyat* (province). The term was introduced after the Mongol invasion. It has been re-introduced again following the demise of the Soviet Union.

'udūl, a. Term used for trustworthy witnesses. Used to denote professional witnesses (notaries), but this technical meaning is not evident in later Bukharan documents.

ūrāgh, t. Official acting as *muḥtasib* among the saiyids of the military.

uskuna, see *sukniyāt*.

ʿushr, a. Tithe (basic land/produce tax of one tenth of produce, payable in kind or in money).

wakālat, a. Status of proxy or attorney, *khaṭṭ-i wakālat*, power of attorney, *wakālatan* (see also *aṣālatan*), acting as attorney for an identified person (*muwakkil*), often a minor or a woman.

wakīl, a. Proxy, attorney.

walad, a. Son (of), introducing the patronym.

wāqif, a. Endower, person who makes an endowment (*waqf*).

waqfiyya, a. or *waqf-nāma*, a-p., endowment deed.

waṣī, a. Guardian (for a minor, frequently an orphan); *waṣāyatan*, acting as guardian for one's ward in a legal transaction.

waṯīqa, a. Term for a private legal document.

wilāyat, a. Largest territorial administrative unit, province. See also *tūmān*.

wizārat-panāh, a-p. „Refuge of the vizierate", term used as address in letters, petitions, and official documents for the *qūsh-begī*. This was his official title.

yārlīgh, t. Decree issued by the ruler.

zamīn, p. Land, arable or garden or built.

zamīn-i dahyakī, p. Land from which the tithe is due (basic tax - one tenth of produce).

zamīn-i mamlaka, government land.

zamīn-i milk, private property (normally owing the *kharāj* as basic tax).

zamīn-i ḥurr-i khāliṣ, private property exempted from all taxes.

APPENDIX II

Examples of documents in the BOB collection

1. *Inventory number 16/6.*

Decree issued by the Shibanid ruler Naurūz Aḥmad Khān to prince Muḥammad Hāshim Sulṭān, 963/1556.

1 He is the Judge, the Knowing One.

2 Abū l-Ghāzī Nawrūz Aḥmad Bahādur Khān, Our word.[1]

3 He is the Ruler, the Giver of gifts.[2]

Dear brother, graced with felicity, gifted with the favor-bestowing

4 regards of the Majesty[3], Muʿizz ad-Dīn

5 Muḥammad Hāshim Sulṭān[4], hoping for royal favors, know that We have issued the order

6 that His Excellency, the abode of the saiyids' nobility[5], the mansion of the sharia, the one who carries high duties in the sublime buildings of Islam, the embodiment of supreme judgeship, to whom

---

[1] The intitulation formula *sözimiz* is used frequently in Mongol and post-Mongol decrees. The Russian translation most frequently used is *slovo nashe*. See M.A. Usmanov, *Zhalovannye akty Dzhuchieva ulusa*, 186-7.

[2] This formula is written in the right margin, *malik-i mannān*.

[3] Taking *ḥaḍrat* to refer to God here. (Translator's note.)

[4] As is well known, the title *sulṭān* was used for all male members of the ruling house in the Shibanid domains.

[5] The formula used here is evidence that the man in question is a saiyid himself.

7 the mighty and the noble turn, of excellent descent, respected far and wide,[6] true follower and servant of the sharia,

8 [Amīr Akram ad-Dīn Muḥammad Shafī‘][7], may God's blessings on him last, shall sit on the right hand side, [the side of the saiyids], and nobody shall

9 sit higher than he. Now, seeing this decree[8], you, dear brother, shall act

10 accordingly and place nobody of the descendants of Saiyid Ata[9] and nobody else higher than the aforementioned high person

11 and consider it your duty to honor and favor him. He[10] cannot be compared to others,

12 We have bestowed extraordinary benefits on him, as you will have found out. Thus,

13 behave in a way that he will be contented with you. He has earned many a right in Our service,

14 he has done Us much good. Let there be no neglect in this respect.

15 This is a sealed decree, given in the month of Sha‘bān, 963.[11]

---

[6] The term *ḥasīb* is used for nobility of descent as well as merit, *ḥasab* (in that case, merit) is sometimes opposed to *nasab* (descent).

[7] The name written on the right margin.

[8] In Timurid chancery practice, the term *nishān* „decree" is - in documents written in Turkī - used only for documents issued by the ruler. See A.P. Grigor'ev, *Mongol'skaia diplomatika*. Leningrad 1978, 63 and 64 (decrees issued by the Timurids Shāhrukh and ‘Umar Shaikh).

[9] Well-known saint dated roughly to the 14th century. His (real or alleged) descendants held important positions in court ceremonies. See Devin DeWeese, „Ata'iyya" in *Encyclopedia Iranica*. Places on ceremonial occasions were given according to strict rules, see: Devin DeWeese, „The descendants of Sayyid Ata and the rank of *naqīb* in Central Asia". - In: *Journal of the American Oriental Society* 115.4 (1995), 611-634. Descendants of Saiyid Ata enjoyed high esteem at many courts of Shibanid appanage and central rulers and were in some cases placed at the highest place to the *left* of the ruler which was considered nobler than the right. (Translator's note.)

[10] Verbal forms and pronouns in the plural referring to the *qāḍī*.

[11] The addressee, Muḥammad Hāshim Sulṭān, is not mentioned in Burton, *Bukharans*; he seems not to be mentioned in Ḥāfiẓ-i Tanīsh, *Sharaf-nāma-yi shāhī*, either (ed. and Russian translation Salakhetdinova, vol. 1, Moskva 1983). He might be related to Hāshim Sulṭān b. Burunduq (who was not a direct descendant of Abū l-Khair and therefore is not included in Burton's list). This Hāshim (who is mentioned in the *Sharaf-nāma*, to be sure) was

(Additional note in the right margin):

1 When your blessed father was still living, Quraish Khwāja, who at first

2 disagreed, later sat below the *qāḍī* [Muḥammad Shafīʿ].

3 Now we have gained certitude [that the *qāḍī*] will always know your advantage.

4 Now act according to the custom established by your father and do not seat anybody

5 higher than the *ḥaḍrat qāḍī*.

2. *Inventory number 17/3.*

Purchase deed, Samarqand, 1116/1704.

1 Deed of sale (*chak*) concerning the place Īskī Fīranj[12], owing the tithe[13].

2 In the name of God, the Merciful, the Compassionate.

3 He is the Owner of everything, from the foundation of the earth to the highest skies[14].

4 Due praise to that Owner whose property deed is „He made usurpation unlawful and permitted trade"[15], and worthy qualities given to that Lord of Lords who,

together with his clan ruling the appanage of Ḥiṣār in present-day Tajikistan and an important ally of Naurūz Aḥmad Khān in the intra-Shibanid struggles. After the death of Naurūz Aḥmad Khān, a member of the Burunduqī clan, Tīmūr Aḥmad, was the pretendant of this faction. See also in E.A. Davidovich, *Korpus zolotykh i serebrianykh monet Sheibanidov, XVI v.* - Moskva 1992. - I have not been able to identify the *qāḍī* Akram ad-Dīn either. (Translator's note.)

[12] Heading written in the left half on top of the document. The place name could not be identified, the reading is conjectural.

[13] The tithe, *dahyak*, is one of a variety of categories arable land (or other landed property) could be classed in. For this category and its corollary, the *kharāj* land *dahdū*, see E.A. Davidovich, „Feodal'nyi zemel'nyi milk v Srednei Azii XV-XVIIIvv.: sushchnost' i transformatsii". (Translator's note.)

[14] Literally, „from the fish to Arcturus", *min as-samak ilā s-simāk*. The zodiacal sign Pisces is however not intended; the „fish" (*samak*) is an allusion to the animal upon which in popular cosmology the earth rests, and Arcturus of course is one of the high-rising stars. (Translator's note.)

5 whenever his service and prescriptions are neglected, deems it necessary to „send prophets with good tidings, graced by His glance“[16], and infinite duration to that Creator who established the well-ordered

6 face of the earth to the benefit of the various classes of His prophet's communities, the scholars, the literati, the pious and God-fearing, the amirs and viziers, and who revived

7 the fruit-bearing lands of the lovers of God with the running water of the canals (*qanawāt*) of wisdom and the fountains of gnosis. And [let] prayers [be offered] for the Prophet who disposes

8 directly, without sale or purchase, through his noble law (*sharī'at*), may God's blessings and peace be upon him, of all people, princes and amirs, as of a plot of land,

9 as long as springs are gushing forth and the land is bearing fruit. And hereafter[17]. This is a document (*dhikr*) giving legal proof and all legally required conditions have been met in it. The following was transacted: This day, 17th Rabī' al-auwal in the year 1116 [month beg. July 4, 1704], the named Yūsuf b. Ḥusain Yār made the legally binding disposition, in his own name and in the name of Niyāz Bībī bint Mu'min Bī, for whom he was acting as fully authorized attorney, in the presence of the deputy *qāḍī* of Islam for the city of Samarqand and its surroundings, may God lengthen his high shade, when he was legally able to do so:

13 I sold, to Jān Fulād Dīwānbīgī b. Qadr Bāy, definitely and in a legally binding way, completely and entirely, three plots of land, my right and property and that of the person for whom I am acting as attorney, situated in the place called

15 Īskī Fīranj, in the *tūmān* Shāwdār of [Samarqand] province. These plots have the following well-defined borders: to the West, they border partly on the White Cliff[18] and on the land

---

[15] This quotation is to be found neither in the Qur'ān nor in the canonical collections of ḥadīth. (Translator's note.)

[16] See preceding note.

[17] In the following, line numbers are not given individually, since the translation could not follow the syntax of the Persian text closely enough to permit this. (Translator's note.)

[18] The name of the place probably is *jar-i safīd*, this may or may not be a proper name. Reading suggested by Florian Schwarz.

called „field of Yūsuf shaikh"[19], partly on Sabuk-tūda and partly on the fields of Bābā Yūlak and partly on the fields called Shamrānī-yi Uyghūr[20]; to the north, on the place called Dū Sāya; to the east, on the place called the Dry Brook (*sā-yi khushk*); to the south, partly on the fields of [the place called] Maidānī, partly on a public alley, and partly to the mosque of the said place, and partly

19 on the fringe of the canal Jūy-i Shaikhān. The borders in each case are clearly marked and well-known. [I sold these lands] together with all rights and benefits of irrigation by their water courses/irrigation system for the sum of one thousand tanga of the type now current, *dah-dū nīm*[21]. Both contracting parties exchanged the equivalents in due manner, the guarantee that the purchaser would be able to take over was given, and the price was fair and corresponded to the market value of the object sold as attested by just assayers of real estate. The contract was made without deceit or fraud and without void clauses.

23 And the mentioned purchaser purchased the mentioned object in the described manner, and he confirmed the described deposition, orally and face to face to the selling party.

And this was transacted in the presence of trustworthy witnesses:

[Various seals, among them a circular one by the *qāḍī*, b. Mīr ʿAbdallāh Mūsāwī. 22 more seals impressed by witnesses. Formula introducing names of further witnesses, probably those who did not have a personal seal: Present were: Names only partly legible.]

---

[19] *Mazraʿa-yi Yūsuf shaikh.*

[20] All readings of placenames are conjectural.

[21] This specification is hard to understand. See, for an instance of a similar specification (*tanga-yi dah sa-ū-nīmī*), O.D. Chekhovich, *Dokumenty k istorii agrarnykh otnoshenii v Bukharskom khanstve*, Tashkent 1954, doc. 10, line 29. - Literally, the expression *dah-dū nīm* means „two and a half in ten", that is, a quarter. A possible explanation would be to refer this to the part of silver in the coins. It is well known that in the last decades of the 17th and well into the 18th century, debased coinage with only 25 to 30% of silver circulated widely. See *Istoriia Uzbekistana, tom iii.* Tashkent 1993, 132. (Translator's note added). - Another explanation would be an exchange rate: 2,5 in 10 (of whatever currency is intended). This second explanation was suggested by Florian Schwarz.

[On the right margin, up to down, a question as for a *fatwā*:]

1 In confidence in the commemoration of His name. What do the imams of Islam say - may Allah have mercy on them all[22] - is this contract valid and legally binding according to the sharia or not? Answer, may God reward you.

3. *Inventory number 335/257.*

„Mortgage". Act handing over *suknīyāt* built on land belonging to an endowment as a pawn in order to obtain a loan, Bukhara, 1301/1883-4.

1 On the 12th of Sha'bān, Ṭāhir Bīk, of dark complexion, tall, son of Qābil Bīk, came to the office of the *dār al-iḥtisāb*[23] in the proud city of Bukhara, to make the following legal and valid deposition, while he was legally able to do so:

4 I have sold, in a legally revocable sale [*bai'-i jā'iz*], to 'Abd al-Karīm Bīk, son of Muqīm Āqsaqāl[24], the complete *suknīyāt*[25] situated on [...][26] of the land belonging to an endowment made for a specified purpose which are my right and my property. This land is located in the place called Ūtrār[27], north of the main canal[28]. To the west, it borders on a public canal, to the north likewise, to the east to the house (*ḥawīlī*) where Shādī Bīk, son of Qābil Bīk, is living, to the south likewise. The borders are all marked by well-known signs.

9 [I sold this] for the sum of 160 silver tanga of good quality, Bukharan coinage, carrying the name of the Commander of the Faithful, God bless him[29]. Both parties have taken possession of the objects exchanged.

---

[22] The word *ajma'īn* which is expected here has been replaced by a shorthand note in a stylized form.

[23] One of the places in Bukhara where notarial documents could be drawn up, see above, chapter „Topography of chanceries", section 1.2, chancery of the *ra'īs*.

[24] In the present document, this is probably the village elder.

[25] See glossary.

[26] The area occupied by these *suknīyāt* cannot be deciphered.

[27] This is the name of a place in the south-western outskirts of Bukhara.

[28] *Rūd.* This is the current name of the main canal which feeds the city of Bukhara.

[29] The title of the ruler is written on top of the document in *elevatio.*

Moreover, the named person made the following deposition:

11 I have taken the mentioned sold object in legal lease, on condition that I pay, at the end of each month, the sum of twenty[30]-three tanga of the kind mentioned above, and he agreed to this.

12 And this was [transacted] in the presence of Muslims.

[Seal, oval, 33x46mm, Muḥammad ʿĀrif Khwāja ṣadr raʾīs b. Mullā ʿAbd al-Muʾmin khwāja ākhund aʿlam 1300 (1882-3).]

[Shorthand note for „Present were“ (*ḥuḍḍār al-majlis*), two names of witnesses following: Muqīm Āqsaqāl, Ismāʿīl Bī „and others“ (*wa-ghairuhum*).]

4. *Inventory number 427/344.*

Act (protocol of an *iqrār*) concerning two plots of land, Nasaf, 1317/1899.

1 [Act concerning] a plot of land of tax-free private property (*milk-i ḥurr*), about a quarter of a *ṭanāb* and three and a half *nīmcha* [this would make 11/16 of a *ṭanāb*][31] in size, [called] „Qāḍī Yaʿqūb“, situated

2 in the quarter of Yūlūm Shaikh, in the [town and] *wilāyat* Nasaf. [Its borders]: to the west, it borders on the lands belonging to the heirs of ʿAbd al-Khāliq, to the north on the edge of a public canal,

3 to the east, on the lands belonging to *ustā*[32] Kamāl, son of *ustā* Ghafūr, to the south, on lands belonging to a *waqf* endowed for a specified purpose. And besides,

[30] The word „twenty“ conjectural (defect in text).

[31] The term *nīmcha* occurs rather frequently as a measure of land in Bukharan documents from the end of the 19th-beginning of the 20th century as a fraction of a *ṭanāb*. It must be smaller than a quarter of a *ṭanāb*. Area size can be indicated in the following way: two *tanāb*, three quarters of a *ṭanāb* and half a *nīmcha*, as in inv.nr. 348/271, 1900. However, in the specialized literature, this term is known only as a measure of weight, see E.A. Davidovich, *Materialy po metrologii Srednei Azii*, Moskva 1970, 97-8.

[32] This term was (and is) used in Central Asia for specialists in a wide variety of professions, but mostly crafts.

4 another plot of land, tax-free private property, about two *ṭanābs* and one quarter and half a quarter [2 and 3/8 of a *ṭanāb* in all], situated in the place mentioned above. [Its borders:]

5 to the west, it borders on the lands belonging to Kamāl-bābā, son of *ustā* Ghafūr, to the north, on the edge of a public canal, to the east, to the land belonging to the heirs of Tūra-Khwāja,

6 to the south, on the lands belonging to ʿAbd al-Faiyāḍ, son of ʿAbd al-Ḥafīẓ. The borders are marked by clear signs. [The land goes together with] all benefits and its irrigation water.

7 In the month of Ṣafar, 1317, master Kamāl, the coppersmith (*misgar*), came to the court house

8 of Nasaf province, and made the following trustworthy, legally binding declaration, while he was legally able to do so:

9 I, making this declaration, sold [*furūkhtam* instead of the habitual *furūkhta-am* used in purchase deeds] in irrevocable sale, in a formal and legally binding way, to the woman called Maḥfūẓa-Āy, daughter of ʿIzm ad-Dīn,

10 completely and entirely the two plots of land described at the beginning of this document, my right and property, for the sum of 5820

11 (five thousand eight hundred and twenty)[33] current tanga, in the coinage of His Majesty, the amir, God's blessings upon him[34]. Both equivalents have been exchanged, guarantee was given to the purchaser that she would have free access to the property,

12 the contract was concluded without deceit or fraud, and without void conditions. And this was in the presence of Muslims.

[Circular seal, 41mm Qāḍī mullā Qawām ad-Dīn khwāja ṣudūr b. Anwar khwāja. 1316 (1898/9).]

[Shorthand sign for the introduction *ḥuḍḍār al-majlis*, „present were", and the names of two witnesses, ʿAbd al-Karīm Āqsaqāl, Muḥammad Āqsaqāl, [...][35] Āqsaqāl „and others".

---

[33] Given both in figures and in words in the text.
[34] The title of the ruler written at the top of the document in *elevatio*.
[35] Name omitted.

5. *Inventory number 445/361.*

Lease of *waqf* lands. Bukhara, 1338/1920.

1 He, the Living One.[36]

2 On Ramadan 17th, 1338, the *waqf* lands of the additional endowment (*waqf-i mā zāda*) to the benefit of the *khānaqāh* of the shaikhs of Chahār Manār, situated in the places called Ghunjārī and Marghāsūn, *tūmān* Sāmijān, and Kūl-i Ādīna, *tūmān* Pīrmast, and Shaikhān and Qalmāq-Rabāṭ, to the north of the main canal, have been separated and given entirely and completely to mullā Shādīmurād, son of Balta-Bāy, in a legal contract of lease. The borders of these holdings are well-known. The lease is valid for seven lunar months from the mentioned date. The price is 45000

6 (forty five thousand) presently current tanga, which is the fair price for seven months. It has further been stated that three thousand tanga should be paid [in advance] for the contract (*maqbūḍ-i ijāra-dārī*)

7 and twelve thousand in cash [in advance], the rest in two instalments of fifteen thousand each. In this manner, the lessee can acquit himself of his obligations.

8 He has agreed to this. And this was in the presence of Muslims.

[Oval seal, 39x47cm: Qāḍī mullā ʿIẓām ad-Dīn ṣadr raʾīs b. mullā Muḥammad ʿĀrif ṣadr muftī. 1337 (1918/9).]

[Shorthand sign for *ḥuḍḍār al-majlis*, „Present were". No names of witnesses.]

Additional act to the previous document. Inventory number 445a/361a. Undated.[37]

1 He, the Living One.

[36] The invocation is indicated only by a shorthand sign in form of a line symbolizing this formula. For the use of this symbolic line in private documents from Transoxiana see: Mīrzā Badīʿ Dīwān, *Majmaʿ al-arqām*. Moskva 1981, text, 21.

[37] Text written on the right margin of the main document, lines narrower: two lines to one.

2 Let it not be hidden that the lessee mentioned in the [main] document leased the holdings

3 mentioned in the [main] document for another term[38], at an increase of 8000, so that the overall price is

4 63000 (sixty three thousand) presently current tanga.[39]

5 It has been stated that one thousand tanga in this addition would be given [in advance] for the contract, eighteen thousand

6 in cash as general prepayment, and that the remainder would be paid

7 in two instalments of twenty-two thousand tanga each.
[Oval seal, identical to the one imprinted beneath the main document.]

---

[38] Duration of term not indicated.

[39] There is something wrong with the figures. The increase should be 18000, since the first contract cost 45000 and the second one 63000.

BIBLIOGRAPHY

Abduraimov, M.A.: *Ocherki agrarnykh otnoshenii v bukharskom khanstve v XVI - pervoi polovine XIX veka.* Tom I, Tashkent 1966.

Andreev, M.S. and O.D. Chekhovich: *Ark (kreml') Bukhary.* Dushanbe 1972.

Astanova, G.Yu.: „Arkhiv kushbegi - vazhnyi istochnik". - In: *Obshchestvennye nauki v Uzbekistane* 1985 no. 7

Babadjanov, B.; A. Muminov; J. Paul: *Schaibanidische Grabinschriften.* Wiesbaden 1997.

Bosworth, Clifford E.: *The* New *Islamic Dynasties.* Edinburgh 1996.

Bregel, Yuri: *The Administration of Bukhara under the Manghits and some Tashkent manuscripts.* Bloomington 2000 (Papers on Inner Asia : 34).

Bregel, Yuri: *Bibliography of Islamic Central Asia.* 3 vols. Bloomington 1995.

Bregel, Yuri: Art. „Koshbegi" in *Encyclopedia of Islam.*

Bregel, Yuri: *Notes on the Study of Central Asia.* Bloomington 1996 (Papers on Inner Asia : 26).

Bukharskii vakf XIII v. Faksimile, izdanie teksta, perevod s arabskogo i persidskogo, vvedenie i kommentarii A.K. Arendsa, A.B. Khalidova, O.D. Chekhovich. Moskva 1979.

Bulgakov, P.G.: „Formuliary dokumentov po chastnomu pravu." - In: *Materialy po istorii Srednei Azii.* Tashkent 1991

Burton, Audrey: *The Bukharans.* Surrey 1997.

Chekhovich, O.D.: *Bukharskie dokumenty XIVv.* Tashkent 1965.

Chekhovich, O.D.: *Dokumenty agrarnykh otnoshenii v Bukharskom khanstve. Vyp. I: akty feodal'noi sobstvennosti na zemliu XVII-XVIII vv.* Tashkent 1954. (all published)

Chekhovich, O.D. „O diplomatike i periodizatsii sredneaziatskikh aktov." - In: *Istochnikovedenie i tekstologiia srednevekovogo Blizhnego i Srednego Vostoka.* Moskva 1984, 224-230.

Chekhovich, O.D.: „Ob aktovykh materialakh po istorii Bukhary". - In: *Istoricheskie zapiski* 16, Moskva 1945

Davidovich, E.A.: „Feodal'nyi zemel'nyi milk v Srednei Azii XV - XVIII vv.: sushchnost' i transformatsii" . - In: *Formy feodal'noi sobstvennosti i vladeniia na Blizhnem i Srednem Vostoke.* Bartol'dovskie chteniia 1975g. Moskva 1979, 39-62.

Davidovich, E.A.: *Korpus zolotykh i serebrianykh monet Sheibanidov, XVI v.* Moskva 1992.

Davidovich, E.A.: *Materialy po metrologii Srednei Azii.* Moskva 1970.

DeWeese, Devin: Art. „Ata'iyya" in *Encyclopedia Iranica.*

DeWeese, Devin: „The descendants of Sayyid Ata and the rank of *naqīb* in Central Asia." - In: *Journal of the American Oriental Society* 115.4 (1995), 611-634.

DeWeese, Devin: „The eclipse of the Kubravīyah in Central Asia". - In: *Iranian Studies* 21 (1-2), 45-83.

Egani, A.A. and O.D. Chekhovich: „Regesty sredneaziatskikh aktov." - In: *Pis'mennye pamiatniki Vostoka (Ezhegodnik)* 1974 (1981), 47-57, 305-336; 1975 (1982), 34-51, 277-317; 1976-7 (1984), 105-110, 321-362; 1978-9 (1987), 57-63, 294-345.

Fekete, Lajos: *Bevezetés a hodoltság török diplomatikijába.* Budapest 1926.

Fragner, Bert G.: „Social and internal economic affairs". - In: *Cambridge History of Iran* 6. Cambridge 1986, 491-567.

Grigor'ev, A.: *Mongol'skaia diplomatika XIII-XIV vv. (Chingizdiskie zhalovannye gramoty).* Leningrad 1978.

Ḥāfiẓ-i Tanīsh: *Sharaf-nāma-yi shāhī*. Ed. and Russian translation A. Salakhetdinova (*Kniga shakhskoi slavy*). Moskva 1983.

Horst, Heribert: *Die Staatsverwaltung der Großselǧūqen und Ḫorazmšāhs*. Wiesbaden 1964.

Istoriia narodov Uzbekistana, vol. 3. Tashkent 1993.

Ishanov, A.: *Bukharskaia Narodnaia Sovetskaia Respublika*. Tashkent 1969.

Islam. Èntsiklopedicheskii slovar'. Moskva 1991.

Ivanov, P.P.: *Arkhiv khivinskix khanov XIX v.: Issledovanie i opisanie dokumentov s istoricheskim vvedeniem*. Leningrad 1940.

Ivanov, P.P.: *Khoziaistvo dzhuibarskikh shaikhov*. Moskva 1954.

Kazakov, B.: „Analyse structurelle des actes de *waqf* provenant d'Asie Centrale, XIIIe-début XXe siècle (dans la perspective de l'établissement de modèles pour banques de données). - In: *Cahiers d'Asie Centrale* 7 (1999), 211-232.

Kazakov, B.: *Dokumental'nye pamiatniki Srednei Azii*. Tashkent 1987.

Kazakov, B.: „Dokumenty mecheti Mir-Tabib." - In: *Bartol'dovskie chteniia* 1990 (tezisy dokladov), Moskva 1990, 35-37.

Kazakov, B.: „Kollektsiia istoricheskikh dokumentov Bukharskogo Gosudarstvennogo muzeia." - In: *Iz istorii kul'turnogo nslediia Bukhary*. Tashkent 1990, 62-78.

Kazakov, B.: „Opyt opisaniia aktov." - In: *Materialy soveshchaniia po vostochnoi arkheografii*. Moskva 1990, 84-7.

Kazakov, B.: „Vidy sredneaziatskikh aktov". - In: *Pamiatniki istorii i kul'tury Bukhary*. Bukhara 1995, 71-6.

Kratkii katalog sufiiskix proizvedenii iz sobranii Instituta Vostokovedeniia Akademii Nauk Respubliki Uzbekistan (Beruni). Berlin 2000.

Kügelgen, Anke v.: *Inszenierung einer Dynastie: Geschichtsschreibung unter den frühen Mangiten Bucharas (1747-1826).* Unpublished *Habilitationsschrift*, Bochum 1999.

Kügelgen, Anke v.; Michael Kemper, Dmitriy Yermakov (eds.): *Muslim Culture in Russia and Central Asia from the 18th to the Early 20th Centuries.* Berlin 1996 (Islamkundliche Untersuchungen : 200).

Kügelgen, Anke v.; Michael Kemper, Allen J. Frank (eds.): *Muslim Culture in Russia and Central Asia from the 18th to the Early 20th Centuries. Vol. 2: Inter-Regional and Inter-Ethnic Relations.* Berlin 1998 (Islamkundliche Untersuchungen : 218).

Kügelgen, Anke v.; Michael Kemper, Aširbek Muminov (eds.): *Muslim Culture in Russia and Central Asia. Vol. 3: Arabic, Persian and Turkic Manuscripts (15th - 19th Centuries).* Berlin 2000 (Islamkundliche Untersuchungen : 233).

Lappo-Danielevskii, A.S.: *Ocherk russkoi diplomatiki chastnykh aktov.* Petrograd 1920.

Lunin, B.V.: *V.V. Bartol'd.* Toshkent 1970.

Lunin, B.V.: *Istoriografiia obshchestvennykh nauk v Uzbekistane.* Tashkent 1974.

McChesney, Robert: „The amirs of Central Asia in the XVIIth century." - In: *Journal of the Economic and Social History of the Orient* 26 (1983), 33-70.

McChesney, Robert: Art. „Shibanids" in *Encyclopedia of Islam.*

Mīr Muḥammad Amīn-i Bukhārī: *'Ubaidallāh-nāma.* Russian translation A.A. Semenov (*Ubaidulla-nama*). Tashkent 1957.

Mīrzā Badī' Dīwān: *Majma' al-arqām.* Ed. A.B. Vil'danova. Moskva 1981.

Mu'īn al-fuqarā: *Kitāb-i mullā-zāda.* Lithographed edition, Novaia Bukhara 1904; ed. Gulchīn-i Ma'ānī, Tehran 1339 HSh/1952.

Paul, Jürgen: „Le village en Asie Centrale aux XVe et XVIe siècles." - In: *Cahiers du Monde Russe et Soviétique* 32 (1991), 9-17.

Richard, Jean: „La conversion de Berke et les débuts de l'islamisation de la Horde d'Or." - In: *Revue d'Etudes Islamiques* 35 (1967), 173-184.

Roemer, Hans-Robert: *Staatsschreiben der Timuridenzeit: Das Šaraf-nāmä des 'Abdallāh Marwarīd in kritischer Auswertung.* Wiesbaden 1952.

Schwarz, Florian: *„Unser Weg schließt tausend Wege ein". Derwische und Gesellschaft im islamischen Mittelasien im 16. Jahrhundert.* Berlin 2000 (Islamkundliche Untersuchungen : 226).

Semenov, A.A.: „Bukharskii traktat o chinakh i zvaniiakh." - In: *Sovetskoe Vostokovedenie* 5 (1948), 137-153.

Semenov, A.A.: *Ocherk pozemel'no-podatnogo i nalogovogo ustroistva b. bukharskogo khanstva.* Tashkent 1929.

Stern, Samuel M.: *Fatimid Decrees. Original documents from the Fatimid chancery.* London 1964.

Troitskaia, A.L.: *Katalog arkhiva kokandskix khanov XIX veka.* Moskva 1968.

Usmanov, M.A.: *Zhalovannye akty Dzhuchieva ulusa.* Kazan' 1979.

Yaḥyā al-Bākharzī: *Awrād ul-aḥbāb wa fuṣūṣ al-ādāb,* ed. Īraj Afshār, Tehran 1345 HSh/1967.

Zajączkowski, A. and A. Reychman: *An outline history of Ottoman diplomatic/Zarys dyplomatyki osmańsko-tureckiej.* Warszawa 1955.

Zajączkowski, A. and A. Reychman: Art. „Diplomatics" in *Encyclopedia of Islam.*

REPRODUCTIONS

Document 1: Decree issued by Naurūz Aḥmad Khān, 1556 92
Document 2: Purchase deed, Samarqand, 1704 94
Document 3: „Mortgage“, Bukhara, 1883 98
Document 4: Act (*iqrār*), Nasaf, 1899 100
Document 5: Lease of *waqf* lands, Bukhara, 1920 102

Document 1 (1556)

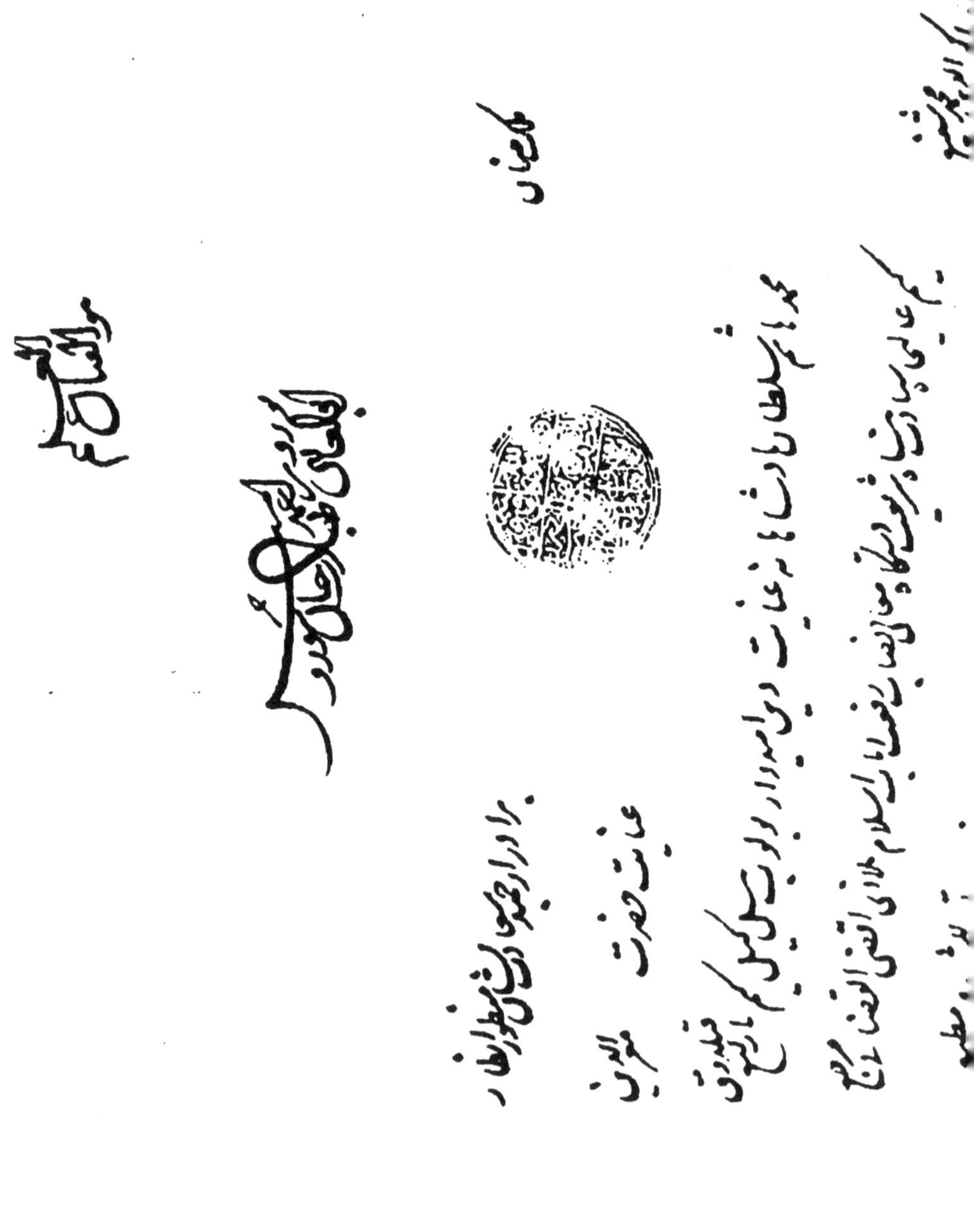

Document 2a (1704)

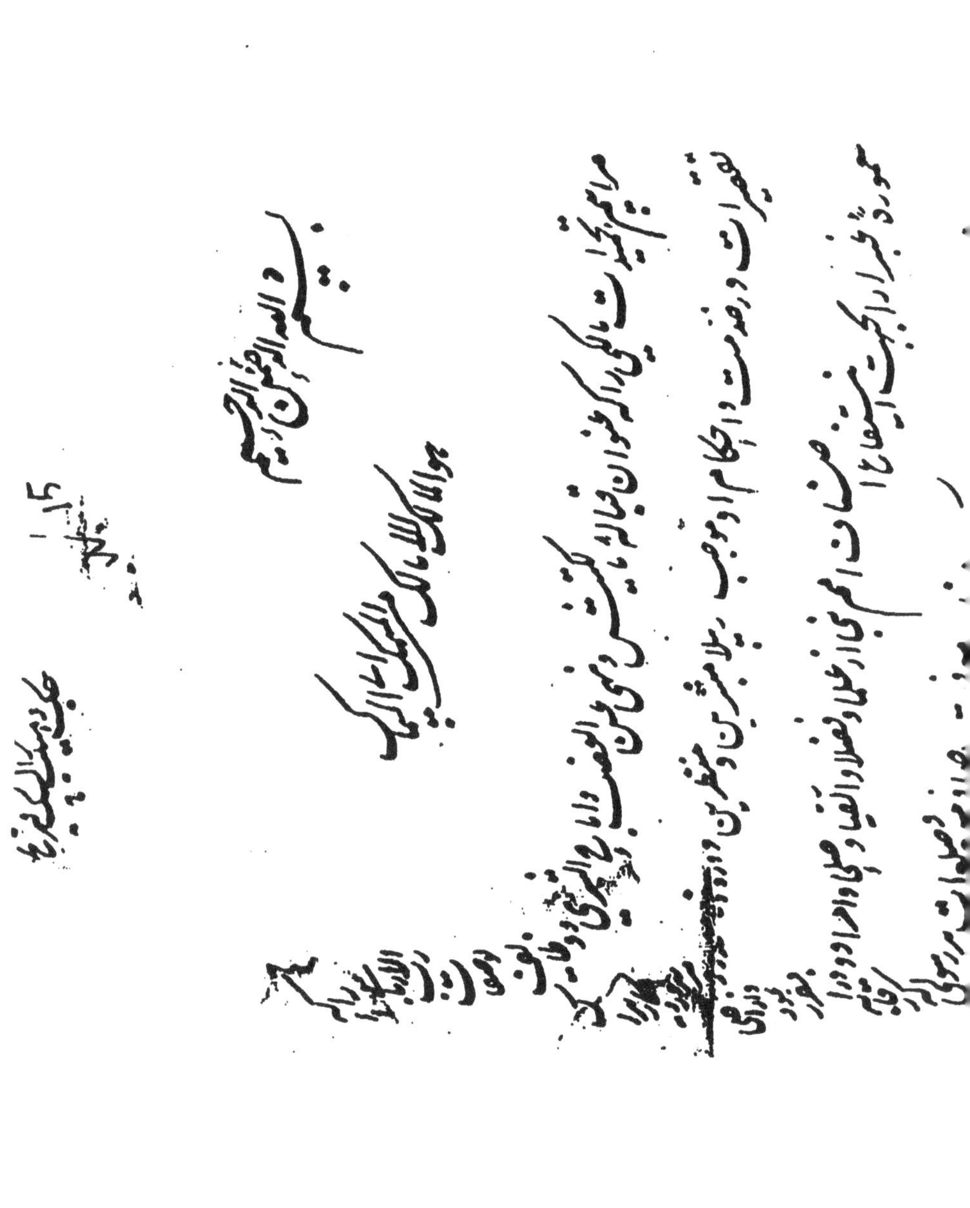

ارباب محبت را القبوات جاریة حکمت و بنای معرفت احیا فرمود صلوات بر روح [illegible]
کافة الوری [illegible] بسلاطین و امرا [illegible] و وسیله [illegible] و تحفه [illegible] تربیت او صلی الله علیه وسلم
مادام العیون جاریة و ارض نامیة اما بعد این ذکر بیت شرعی و جمیع شرایط صحت در وی
مشتمل بر بیان آنکه در تاریخ بیست [illegible] ربیع الاول بود که اقرار صحیح معتبر شرعی کرد بحضور
نایب شرعی قاضی اسلام بلده سمرقند و توابع آن مد ظله العالی [illegible]
و نیز وکیل مطلق عام شرعی بود از قبیل [illegible]
[illegible]
[illegible] قطعه زمین [illegible]

Document 2b (1704)

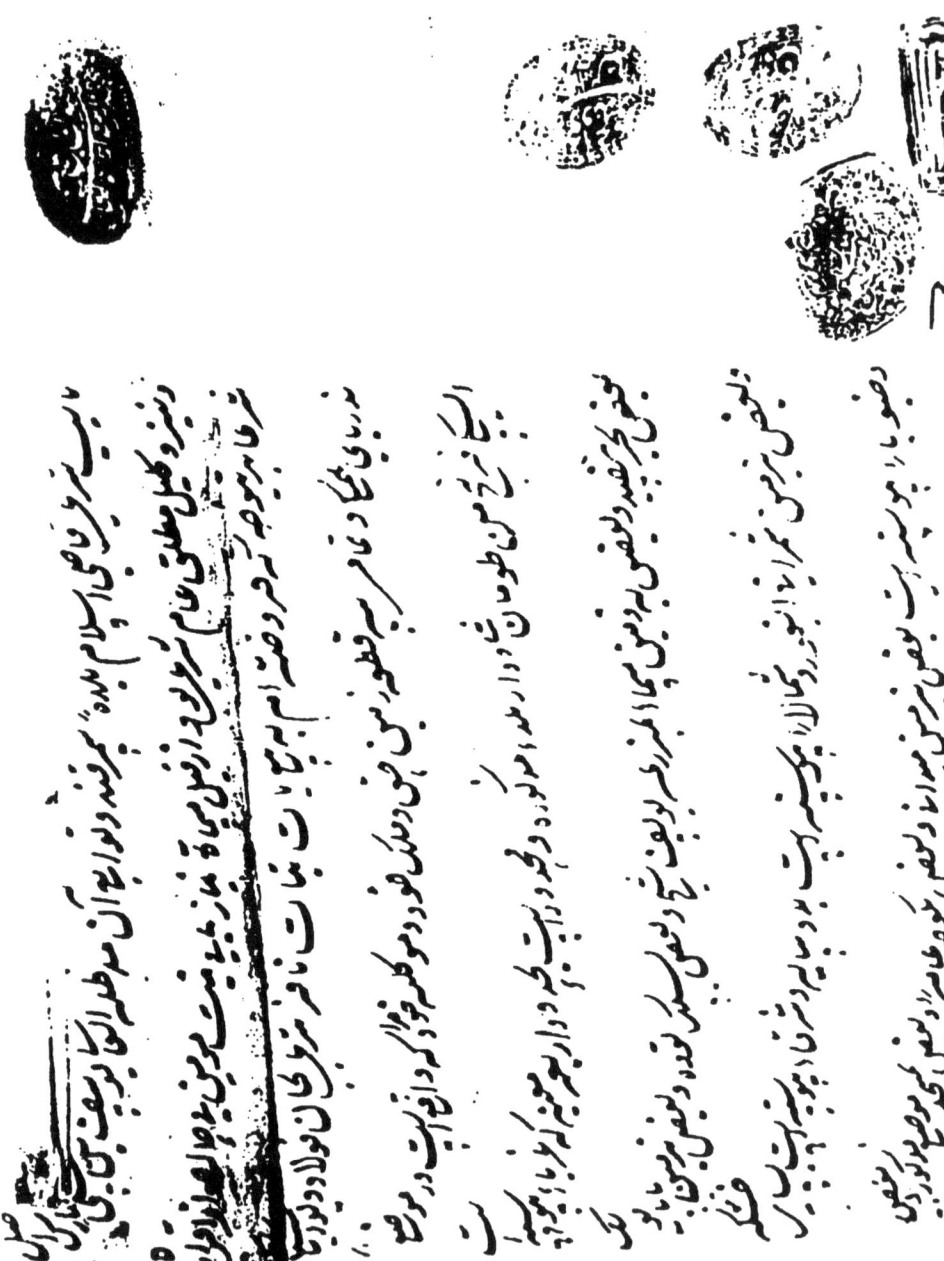

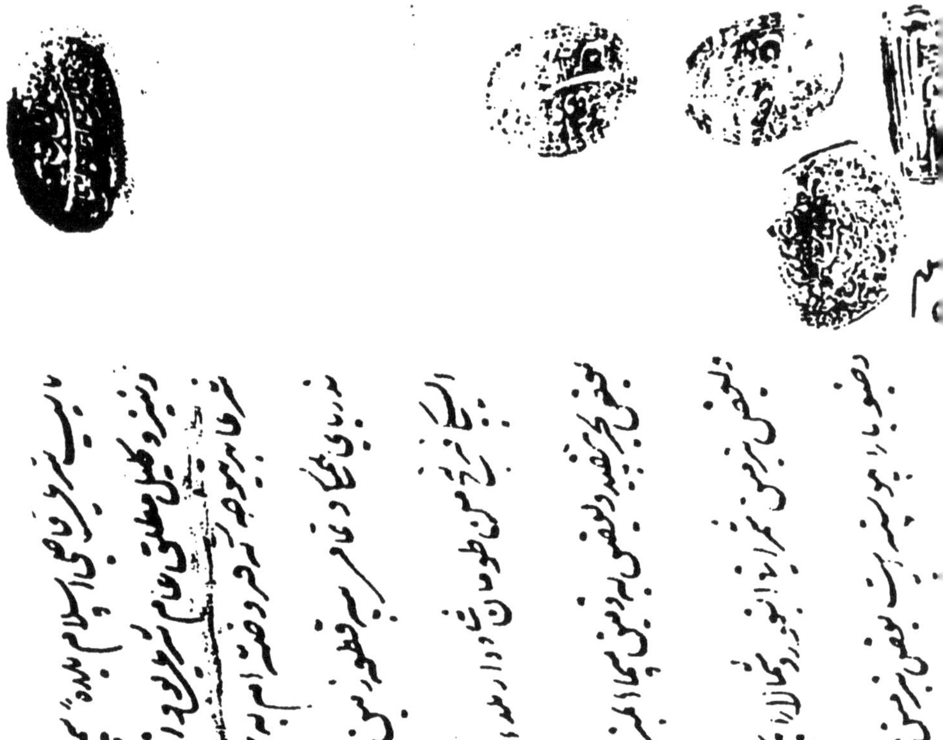

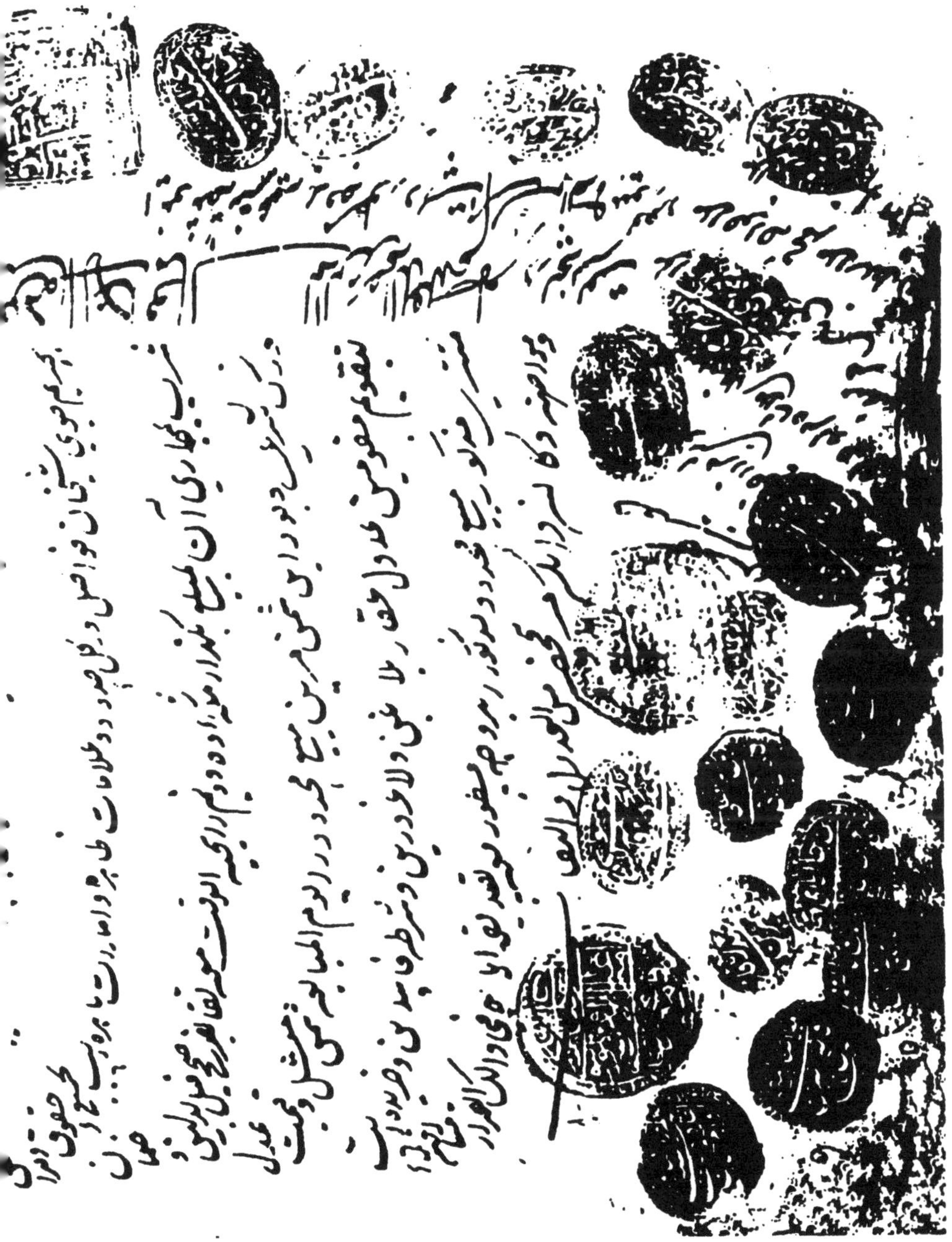

Document 3 (1883)

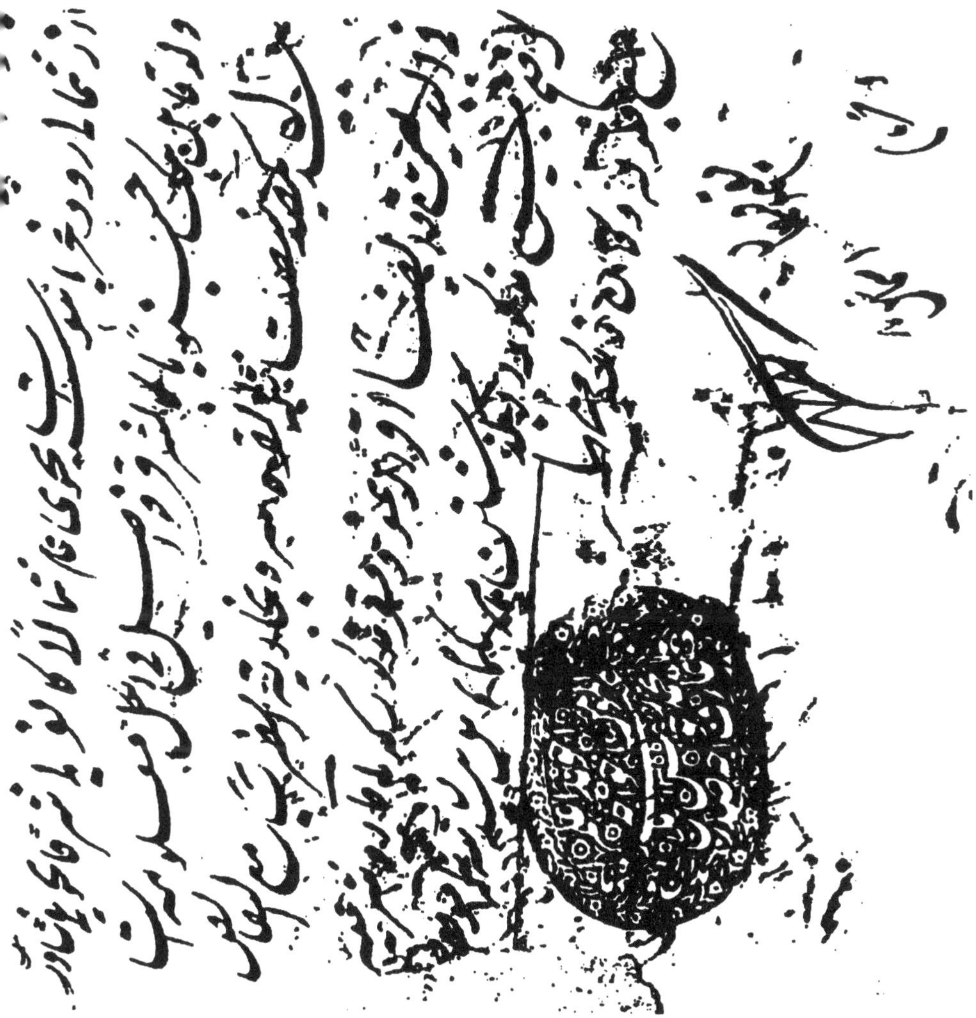

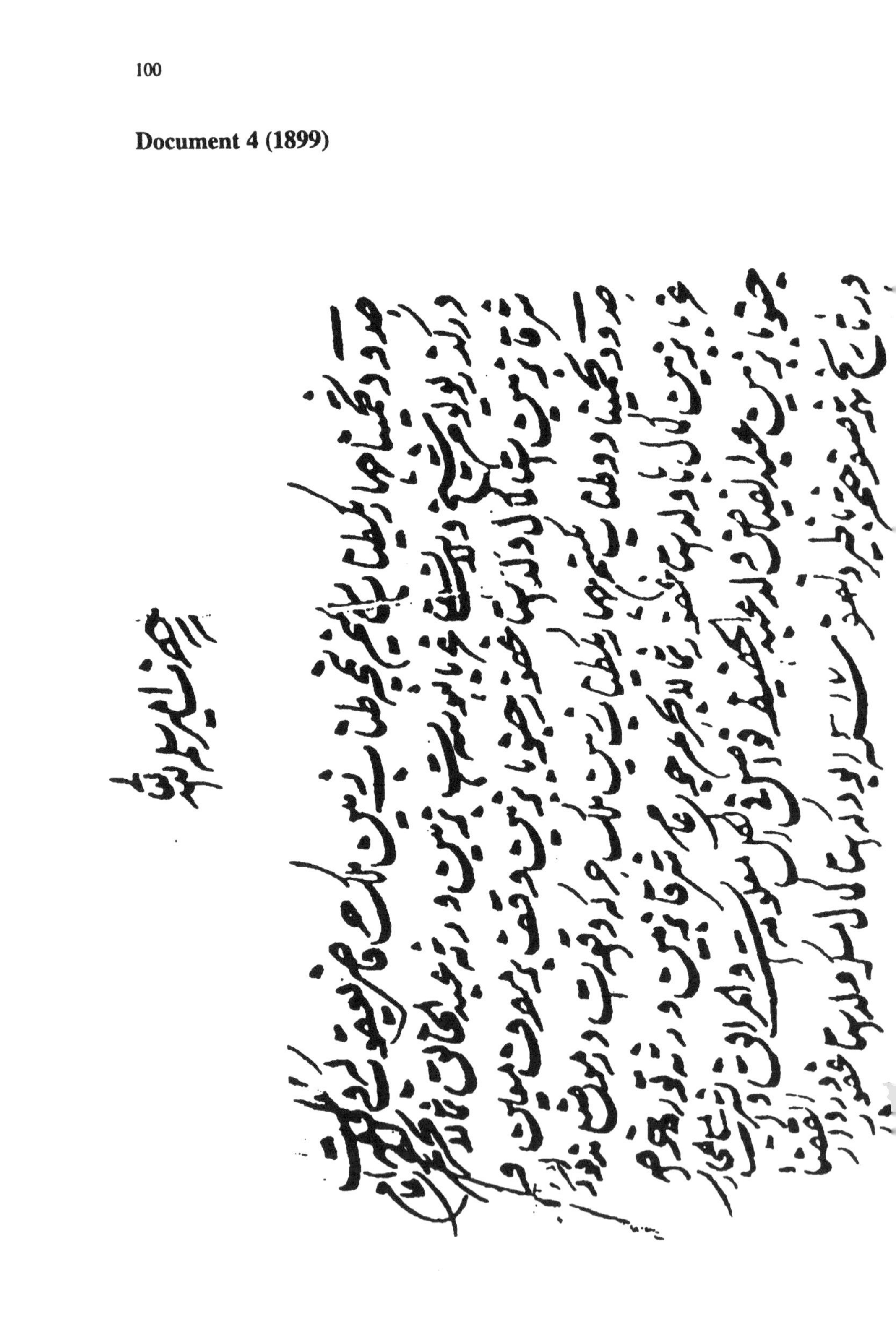

Document 4 (1899)

Document 5 (1920)

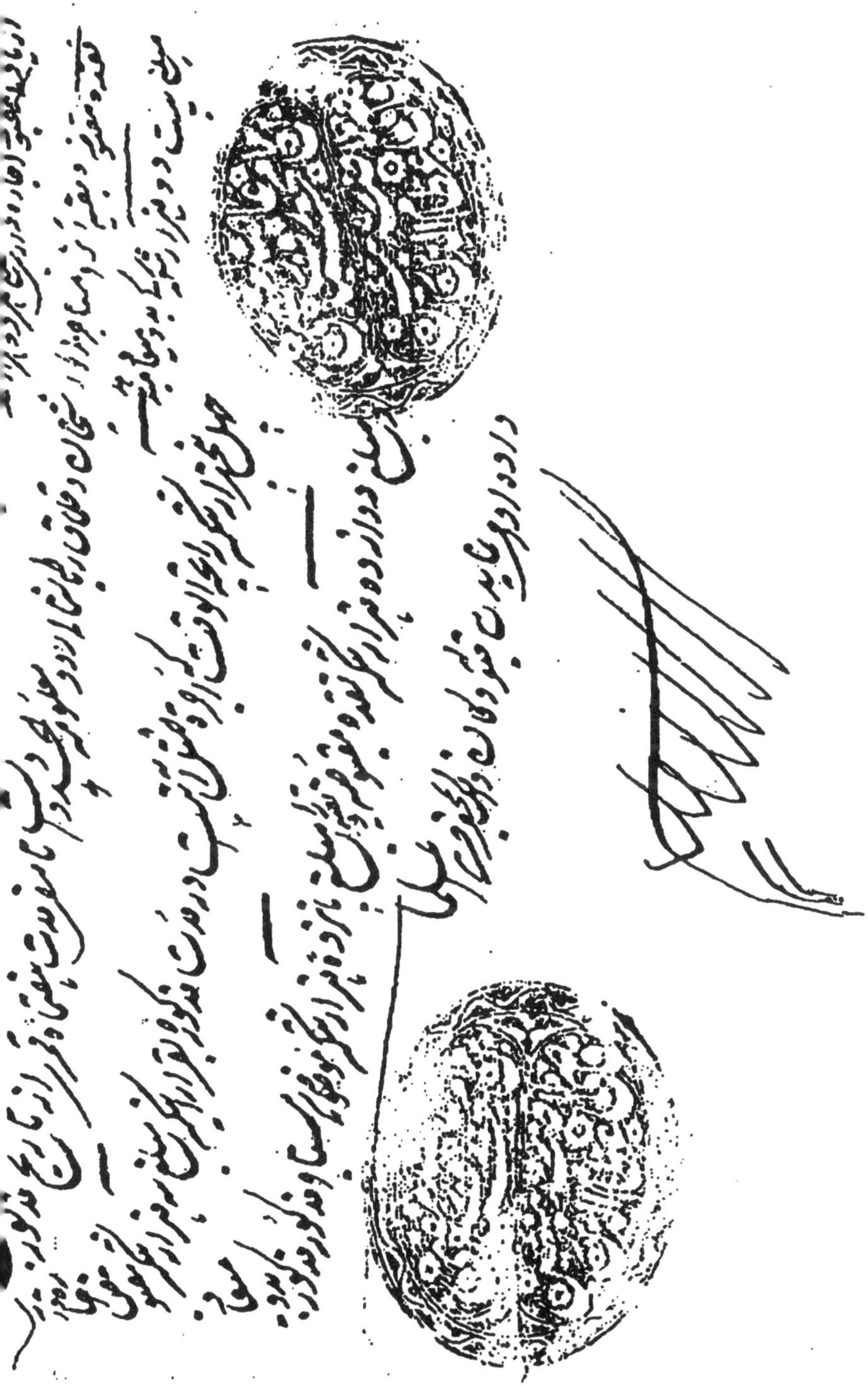

Bei Fragen zur Produktsicherheit wenden Sie sich bitte an:
If you have any questions regarding product safety,
please contact:

Walter de Gruyter GmbH
Genthiner Straße 13
10785 Berlin
productsafety@degruyterbrill.com